THE
HOLLYWOOD
RULES

THE HOLLYWOOD RULES

What You Must Know To Make It in the Film Industry

Anonymous

Fade In: Books
A Division of Fade In: Magazine
www.fadeinonline.com

Fade In: Books
A Division of Fade In: Magazine
www.fadeinonline.com

Fade In: books may be purchased for educational, business or sales promotional use.
For information, please call (800)646-3896.

Library of Congress Cataloging-in-Publication Data is available upon request.
ISBN 0-9677926-0-6

contents--

WHY YOU NEED
THE HOLLYWOOD RULES

Everybody wants to be in the movies. *Everybody*. Ask your plumber if he'd rather root drain pipes or appear in the next Spielberg film, and you can bet he'll toss his monkey wrench in a New York minute. There isn't a neurosurgeon in the nation who, if you picked *his* brain, wouldn't be able to give you at least one idea for a movie he's *convinced* will gross a $100 million domestic.

From Valdez, Alaska to Tierra del Fuego; from the Norwegian fjords to the Australian outback; from the Russian steppes to the Amazon rainforest; there isn't a rice farmer, business mogul, housewife, bushman, lion tamer, tax collector, nuclear physicist, rickshaw driver or professional assassin who, in his/her heart of hearts, doesn't want to be in The Business.

Talk about competition!

Fortunately, most people don't pursue their Hollywood dreams. They content themselves with their day-to-day jobs, with minivans, Little League and waiting for the next big sale at Wal-Mart. Oh, sure, maybe they watch *Access Hollywood* and subscribe to *Entertainment Weekly*. They might even jot down their idea of a sure-fire Academy Award-winner now and then. But to actually hurl themselves into the boiling cauldron of Tinseltown?

Still, there are more than enough people who are driven by dreams of fame and fortune – not to mention the right of final cut – to make this the most competitive business in the world.

How competitive? Put it this way: Every year, thousands of bright, educated, good-looking young men and women don't toil as low-paid waiters and valets for a chance to be *accountants*. Tens of thousands of people don't stay up 'til dawn hunched over their computer keyboards writing *toothpaste ads* on the off-chance that one might actually sell. Otherwise sane men and women haven't been known to beg, borrow, and max out their credit cards for a chance to break into *VCR repair*.

In other words, it's not just raw numbers we're talking about here – and they *are* significant. It's the *desire*, the *need* people have to get into the entertainment business that makes the competition so fierce, and success so elusive. In no other industry are people so willing to degrade, prostitute, and humiliate themselves for even the smallest scrap of film work. Ask any supermodel.

And why not? Show business is the only industry in human creation in which you get to play God by creating other worlds. Making movies allows you to live lives other than your own, to give meaning to an often-meaningless existence, and to guarantee yourself a happy ending. And if you're exceedingly good at what you do, you get paid obscene amounts of money, are lavished with respect and adoration, have access to hordes of exceptionally attractive young men and/or women, and you get to hang out with people you see on TV!

Who wouldn't want to be a part of that?

Unfortunately, despite the growing number of motion picture production companies, independent film operations, TV networks, cable channels, and multinational multimedia entities, there are still not nearly enough creative openings to go around. For example, every year the Writers Guild of America-West registers over 30,000 screenplays. Yet approximately 300 movies are actually produced and released by both studios and independents per annum. The recent creation of the Fox, UPN and WB networks may have added many extra hours of programming a week to prime time, but the proliferation of news-oriented programs like NBC's *Dateline* and ABC's *20/20* and *Prime Time Live* has left the number of dramatic and/or comedy shows on the air at roughly the same level as a decade ago. This means the process of breaking into show business remains just as painfully difficult as it's ever been.

Hence the Hollywood Rules.

Some say that the one rule in Hollywood is that there *are* no rules. Well, They are wrong. It's true that there is no trade school or professional academy that will grant you your license to make movies – every writer, director, actor, agent, and caterer has his/her own individual path to success. But there is a list of "conventions" that exists, and, if properly adhered to, can significantly smooth that otherwise rocky road to a career in entertainment. While there's no substitute for talent and plain old perseverance, there's also no excuse for not knowing how to handle yourself in a pitch meeting, or for acting like an ass when meeting a Really Big Star. Hollywood is held together by a very delicate yet complex social fabric, and the surest way to make it to the inside is to know what's expected of you – and to behave accordingly.

To violate these rules is to mock the Gods themselves.

WHAT ARE THE HOLLYWOOD RULES?

The *Hollywood Rules* are not tricks. They are not about manipulation or subterfuge. The *Hollywood Rules* will not get a talentless hack a job at Paramount, or sell a four-hour-long musical about the invention of Spam to Universal for $5 million.

The *Hollywood Rules* are your friends in the business. They're your mentors. Your gurus. Your tirelessly loyal Virgil here to guide you through the countless circles of Hollywood Hell. Most important of all, the *Hollywood Rules* are your "protectors." They exist not to constrict you, but to make you feel *comfortable* in situations you would otherwise find alien and intimidating. By knowing and following the *Hollywood Rules*, you can relax and let your true brilliance shine through.

At this point, you're probably asking yourself, "Since when has Hollywood respected conformity? Haven't the Big Players always been rule *breakers*, nonconformists, troublemakers?" After all, from the old studio bosses like Harry Cohn, stars like Joan Crawford, and directors like Erich von Stroheim to today's Roseanne, Joel Silver, and Joe

Eszterhas, hasn't Hollywood always rewarded people who are difficult, rude, or downright abusive?

The answer is No. Hollywood *tolerates* unprofessional behavior from people who have already established themselves as marketable entities with a string of successful projects. Only once you reach a certain status – when you become a "name brand" – can you even think about acting like an egomaniacal jerk. This is because a solid track record will lead the Hollywood power brokers to believe you can deliver the goods *despite* being a complete ass.

As you'll probably notice, most of the *Hollywood Rules* included in this book are designed for *creative* talent – namely, writers, directors, and producers. On a professional level, they're designed to help you deal with studio honchos, development executives, stars, agents, and other people who are in a position to help you realize your artistic vision. *The Hollywood Rules* for actors are enough to fill another book. But most of the Rules still apply, and actors and actresses can certainly benefit just as much from the "social" *Hollywood Rules* – such as how to make the most of Hollywood parties – as those of you to whom this book is primarily addressed.

To make this book work for you, it's important to read and apply *all* the *Hollywood Rules*, not just those you find relevant at the moment. Chances are, your Big Break will present itself in a form you've never encountered before, and at the moment you're most vulnerable. By knowing and understanding *all* the *Hollywood Rules*, you'll be ready to take advantage of any opportunity that develops; to feel calm and confident in even the most unusual and bizarre of circumstances.

So take the *Hollywood Rules* to heart. Trust them. Embrace them. Utilize the *Hollywood Rules* and Hollywood will quickly embrace you.

HOLLYWOOD'S BEST-KEPT SECRETS

If you tried to discover all the *Hollywood Rules* on your own, it would probably take you well over ten years. Ten long, painful and frustrating years – and that's if you're good. Many people take much longer to fully realize how the Industry operates. Some people never learn at all. They're called *office temps*.

We've compiled these rules from both our own experiences in the film industry since the mid-1980s, plus those of the dozens of producers, directors, screenwriters, studio executives and agents with whom we work on a daily basis.

Strangely, most industry insiders are reluctant to share this knowledge with outsiders. Or maybe not so strange...for Hollywood is the most paranoid town in the world. You think East Berlin was bad at the height of the Cold War? That's nothing compared to the Disney commissary. Jobs worth hundreds of thousands even millions of dollars annually can disappear with just one poor opening weekend. The decision to buy or pass on a screenplay which took its writer months to create can hinge on something as capricious as whether Studio Exec X got laid the previous night.

With so much at stake, and with so little that's tangible to hold onto, people who find a system of truths that actually *works* will guard it with their lives. The last thing they want is some young upstart threatening their livelihoods – not to mention their really primo parking spaces.

So why are we sharing the *Hollywood Rules* with you? Simple. There just aren't enough good movies being made these days, and we hope you can help. If just one reader of the *Rules* gets the chance to make a film we can enjoy and respect, we've done everyone a service.

And we're sick and tired of *people with talent fucking up because they don't know the Hollywood Rules!* Every day, people like you are torpe-doing their own careers – and our ultimate moviegoing pleasure – out of simple ignorance. There's no excuse for this! It must stop. By bestowing upon you the *Hollywood Rules*, it is our fervent hope that you will avoid the traps and pitfalls which have claimed so many other cre-ative people and allow you to realize the full potential of your abilities.

But there's a catch. Yes, there's a price to pay for this awesome knowl-edge. To paraphrase a line from *Gremlins*, "With the *Hollywood Rules* comes great responsibility." Here it is: By imparting these secrets, we expect you to impart brilliant movies and/or television shows in return. You can't read this book and then sit on your duff and daydream about making it in Hollywood. You can't write one script only to give up when it's rejected. (And don't worry, it *will* be rejected.) You can't make a single 20-minute showcase film and then go back to Chicago or Miami or Dallas or wherever when it doesn't immediately lead to a three-picture deal. You have to *commit* yourself.

Just as important, when you *get* that break, when you *get* that opportunity of a lifetime, don't give us *crap*. We have *enough* crap. We're choking on it. We swear, if you use this awesome knowledge to give us another *B.A.P.S., Jungle 2 Jungle*, or Urkel feature, we'll deport you back to Kansas.

Chapter One

LAYING THE FOUNDATION

Before you can put the *Hollywood Rules* into practice, you have to perfect your most important product: yourself. Luck plays a big factor in making it in this town, but Luck, as they say, favors the ready.

First and foremost, you must *know your craft*. If you intend to be a professional screenwriter, learn everything about screenwriting. Take college courses in the subject at major universities such as USC, UCLA, NYU or Columbia, if you can (although we don't think this is absolutely necessary). Many screenwriting courses are also available on an adult-education or extension basis. Just be selective. A course taught at one of the major Southern California universities is going to be a lot more useful to you than Screenwriting 101 at Southern Missouri State.

There are numerous "How To" books on screenwriting available at retail bookstores, but again, be discriminating. A lot of people who get published don't know what they're writing about. Check the author's credits. Does he or she have any actual *experience* in the movie business? More importantly, does he or she have any actual moviemaking *credits*? As anyone who's gotten a college degree knows, academic knowledge is one thing, but real world experience is quite another.

If you're going to read books on the craft, don't just read one. Compare and contrast several authors' theories and accept those that appear to be common among them all, and make sense in light of what you actually see on the screen. For example, if each author states that most movies have a three-act structure – exposition, development and climax – then it's a good bet it's true. On the other hand, if an author insists that your hero *must* suffer a personal crisis on page 80 exactly, but you've read many produced screenplays in which this didn't happen, then you should probably take this advice with a big old grain of salt.

Which leads us to our next piece of advice. Don't just read books, read screenplays. *Produced* screenplays. Screenplays that actually sold. If you know *anyone* in the Business, chances are he or she can get you a copy of at least one professional, honest-to-God motion picture or television screenplay. If you don't know anyone, then check the Internet for those websites that allow you to download produced screenplays.

But be warned: Often the screenplays on the Net are not final drafts. They may be original or interim drafts that bear only a faint resemblance to the movie that actually wound up on the screen – which, when you think about it, is not such a bad thing. It's often just as instructive to read the author's "original" vision, and understand how it was changed over time, as it is to see how a story ended up after a half-dozen script doctors, producers, directors, and their significant others messed with it.

Here's another caveat: You'll find many famous screenplays available in book form at your local Borders or Barnes & Noble, but while these tomes are great for studying story, dialogue and structure, you must recognize that most are not laid out in standard industry format. You may copy their content but not their style. When professionals see a script that looks like it came out of one of these books, they know it was written by a "wannabe." And that's always a big strike against it. To learn proper format, only reference actual current screenplays.

Another way to learn the craft of screenwriting is to attend courses given at the American Film Institute (AFI) in Los Angeles. This is a somewhat expensive and time-intensive way to gain a Hollywood education, but it's unquestionably a great way to learn from established professionals and to make the kind of early contacts critical to getting your foot in the door once you graduate.

You can also attend weekend seminars given in Los Angeles and other major cities by the so-called "screenwriting gurus," men who make their primary living teaching various theories on the craft. As with screenwriting books, you need to make sure the person you listen to actually has some practical experience. Too many of them have gained their reputations merely as teachers, not *doers*.

There are also weekend-long seminars every few months (like those sponsored by *Fade In:* magazine), primarily in Los Angeles and New York, that feature actual accredited writers, producers, directors, and agents who can offer you advice on everything from writing great dialogue to finding a good entertainment lawyer. Because the speakers at these conferences are industry professionals, their advice can often be far more practical than that offered by other sources, and your chances for gaining an entry into the business is increased by having the opportunity to make contacts. In Hollywood, half the battle *is* who you know.

So far, we've talked primarily about preparing yourself for a career as a professional screenwriter. What if you want to be a director? (And doesn't everybody want to be a director? Heck, if you're not Castro, it's the next best thing to dictatorship.) The educational opportunities for *this* profession are significantly fewer.

If you want to be a great director, again, study screenwriting. More than learning the technical minutiae of camera lenses and film stock, directing is about *storytelling*. And the story always begins with the written word. Many great directors – Francis Ford Coppola, Woody Allen and James Cameron among them – came from a writing background. (You may recall that Coppola won his first Oscar for co-writing 1970's *Patton*, which was directed by Franklin J. Schaffner.) In fact, one of the classic ways of getting a directing gig is to write two or three hit screenplays, then demand the right to personally helm your next feature.

As with screenwriting, you can learn the rudiments of directing through books, seminars, at colleges, or at the AFI. You can also begin by joining or even forming a local theater group. Directing stage plays may not educate you on the technical varieties of the filmmaking process, but it's a great way to learn how to work with actors.

Which brings us to another piece of advice: take acting classes. Since directing is mostly about perspective, it's important to understand and be able to speak to actors, using their own language, in order to get their best performance.

Regardless of training, you must have a reel to show. Unfortunately, your play won't fit in a VCR and can't be viewed at one's leisure, and putting together a reel will cost more than writing a screenplay for yourself to helm, but that five to twenty-thousand dollar investment can pay off when you get to direct your own film. Even if it doesn't lead to a feature, your reel can land you jobs directing commercials and music videos – a very lucrative and highly regarded profession in its own right.

Many of today's top directors such as Ridley Scott (*Alien, Thelma & Louise*), David Fincher (*Seven, The Game*), Michael Bay (*The Rock, Armageddon*), and Simon West (*Con Air*) have a background in advertising and/or music videos, and continue to direct in this arena as well. Although filming the Budweiser frogs or a $1,000 video for Sludge Sandwich might not seem like a way to open many studio doors, a short reel of something is always better than a big crate of nothing. Besides, many of today's commercials and videos are just as technically complex as major studio films, and making music videos may introduce you to many of the same crew members who work in the feature arena. If you can get into either of these fields, even on a fringe basis, it's a solid first step.

And then there's always the home movie. America being a free country – and a Capitalist one at that – means you have a Constitutional right to raise money yourself; to beg, borrow, and steal equipment, and to then shoot a film with your friends, enemies, and anyone else you can get to work for free soft drinks and bagels. Sometimes these films manage to find distribution after being shown at one of the nation's many film festivals. But be warned: Competition for slots in the major festivals like Sundance or Toronto is fierce, and only about one of a hundred submissions actually gets a showing. Of these, fewer than a half-dozen usually generate much interest. In other words, making your own movie with the hopes of establishing a directorial career carries with it enormous financial risk.

Finally, let's talk about how one learns to be a producer.

The problem here is that there are as many definitions of "producer" as there are people carrying that credit. In the old days, the producer was the guy who got the money to get the damn movie made, who shepherded it from concept to screen. Today, the producer can be the person who finds a marketable script, gets a big-name star or director to show some interest in it, then takes the resulting package to a studio that then agrees to finance and/or distribute it. On the other hand, a producer can just be the schmo who waltzes into an exec's office and says, "Let's do a remake of *All Quiet on the Western Front* – only in space!"

In short, producers are dealmakers. They're ambitious people who know lots of other people, and they have the energy, the savvy, the charm, and the vision to pull together all the disparate elements necessary to make a motion picture. (Or perhaps they were merely the first to purchase the rights to some novel that Clint Eastwood wanted to direct.)

Producers tend to come from all sorts of backgrounds. Some come out of marketing, some out of finance. Some are lawyers and – especially today – many are former agents or studio executives. The one thing they have in common is that they *know people* and they have the crucial gift of "schmooze." As a producer, you don't necessarily have to believe in a story idea – you just have to get everyone else to. More than anything else, producing in Hollywood is about creating, cultivating, and exploiting personal contacts.

Now let's assume that you've properly prepared yourself for your eventual Hollywood career. You know your craft. You're good at what you do. Damn good. You have the skills, the talent, and the ambition necessary to be a Hollywood player. All you need now is a gig.

It's time to use the *Hollywood Rules*.

Chapter Two

THE HOLLYWOOD RULES

HOLLYWOOD RULE #1: GET LOCAL

The first mistake many would-be James Camerons make is that they try to establish themselves in Hollywood while living outside of Southern California. And why not? Woody Allen and William Goldman live in New York. Francis Ford Coppola and George Lucas live in the San Francisco area, and they're allowed to write and direct their own films! What with the modern miracles of faxes, e-mail, and Internet video conferencing, you should be able to make films from the Moon, right?

Wrong.

Putting words on paper, bringing that one-in-a-million idea to fruition, is just a small part of establishing and building a film career. In addition to writing, optioning and shooting, there are meetings. Lots of meetings. There are Get-To-Know-You meetings where production execs will sit you down for a half-hour to socialize, talk shop, and generally help them connect a face to the name on the title page. There are Pitch meetings where you'll verbally sell "as-yet-unwritten" story ideas in the hopes of snagging a development deal.

If a friendly producer is looking for a writer to adapt a book she's just purchased, you'll need time to meet about that. If a studio is looking for someone to do the eighteenth rewrite on *Who's the Boss: The Movie*, you ain't gonna get the job without taking a meeting first. If, God willing, your spec script actually sells, you'll meet with development executives about the requisite rewrites. If, by some miracle, you're still on the project after that, you'll meet with the director – *a lot* – and maybe even the stars to discuss *their* script notes.

The fact is, most working writers spend as much time taking meetings as they do actually writing. The same goes for directors and producers, who tend to work the town 24 hours a day. And you can't do any of this by remote control. You have to *be* here. You have to be here to *make* it happen, and you have to be here once it *does* happen.

This is especially true for TV writers. Practically *all* writing for TV dramas and comedies – even those that may be filmed at remote locations in New York or Vancouver – are written right here in SoCal. No one is going to make accommodations to allow you to live anywhere else. Why should they? If you're not willing to make life easy for the producers, there are 10,000 other eager writers who will.

One well-known production V.P. told us the story of a writer from Texas who submitted a spec screenplay that had a great premise, but needed significant work before it could be submitted to a studio. The V.P. called the writer and told him that, if the guy was interested in making movies his career, he really needed to move to Southern California. In the meantime, the V.P. agreed to schedule a conference call the following week to discuss script notes.

The day of the scheduled call arrived. At the appointed time, the V.P.'s secretary entered his office and announced that the writer was here to meet him. "You mean he's on the phone," the V.P. corrected her. "No, he's *here*," the secretary insisted. "He's in the waiting room."

The secretary ushered the young Texan into the V.P.'s office. "You said I needed to move to Los Angeles," he exclaimed. "So I did."

"You *moved*?" the V.P. replied incredulous. "How much money do you have to live on?" "Oh, enough for about three weeks," the young writer confessed.

Naturally, the V.P. was flabbergasted. Nobody rewrites an entire screenplay and sells it *and* gets paid in just three weeks. (Hell, it takes that long for most entertainment lawyers to agree on the definition of net points!) But, having earlier encouraged the young man to move to California, the V.P. felt a moral obligation to help him as best he could.

So for the next three weeks, they worked nonstop, pounding the screenplay into shape. And guess what? At the end of the three weeks, it sold.

Granted, this story is one-in-a-million. But that's true of all Hollywood successes. The point is, by being in Hollywood, the writer could be with the V.P. and spend the time necessary to get the script where it needed to be. Had he stayed in Texas, chances are his script wouldn't have gotten the personal attention it required in order to sell.

Only when you reach the level of a Woody Allen or a William Goldman – again, when you become a "brand name" – can you think about living elsewhere. Until then, you'd best start looking for an apartment within an hour's drive of Studio City.

HOLLYWOOD RULE #2: GIVE 'EM WHAT THEY WANT

If there's one refrain filmmakers always hear from both production executives and critics alike, it's that studios want something *different*! They want something *fresh*! Something *original*! And this is true – but only to an extent.

Just as life itself can only exist within a very narrow range of temperature, pressure, and acidic extremes, so too can a studio screen project only be brought to life when it fits within the thin gap between Too Familiar and Too Weird.

For example, following the surprise success of 1988's *Die Hard*, there was a virtual tidal wave of man-vs.-master criminal movies, all tied to a specific arena. You had *Speed* (*Die Hard* on a bus), *Speed 2* (*Die Hard* on a cruise ship), *Under Siege* (*Die Hard* on a battleship), *Under Siege 2* (*Die Hard* on a train), *Masterminds* (*Die Hard* in a prep school), *Passenger 57* (*Die Hard* on an airplane), *Turbulence* (*Die Hard* on an airplane), *Con Air* (*Die Hard* on an airplane) and *Air Force One* (*Die Hard* on an – oh, yeah...airplane). At this point, studio execs no longer want to see *Die Hard* on much of anything. Likewise, we've recently been through a seemingly never-ending spate of dark and moody serial killer movies inspired by the success of 1991's *The Silence of the Lambs*. We've had *Copycat* and *Seven* and *Kiss the Girls* and *Fallen*.

It's understandably hard for anyone to get excited about another dark and moody serial killer movie. (Even a dark and moody movie about a serial killer on an airplane.)

The worst thing a writer, director or producer can do is try to latch on to a "trend," particularly one that has actually been around for awhile. Remember, the films released next Friday were actually conceived at least two years ago, so the thinking that led to their creation has already moved on to something else. Write another buddy-cop flick or another volcano/earthquake/meteor disaster movie and chances are all you'll elicit are yawns. It doesn't matter how intelligent, well-crafted, or passionate the writing is. If it looks like every other screenplay that's come over the transom in the last month, it ain't gonna get bought.

"But wait!" we hear you cry. "I thought studios love recognizable stories. That's why we got all those *Die Hard* and *Lethal Weapon* clones. That's why they keep dredging up old 1960s TV series. That's why they're still making James Bond movies!"

Yes, that's true. But here's the rub: They can come up with these clones on their own. They don't need your help to revive *That Girl* as a feature film. They already *own* the rights to that – and they can hire their best buddies to pound out the story. The one thing you can bring to the party – in fact, the *only* thing you can bring – is a story that is wholly and completely your own. *That's* what the buyers want. *That's* what they're willing to pay the big bucks for. And *that's* what will get you noticed: Being original...

...Just not too original.

For just as familiarity can be the kiss of death, so can runaway ingenuity. Producers, especially those affiliated with the major studios, are loath to tackle projects that are too far from the mainstream.

For example, there's a subset of spec screenplays we see all the time from fledging writers, which we have deemed New Age. These scripts tend to deal with UFOs, reincarnation, witchcraft, out-of-body experiences and parallel dimensions – usually all at the same time. They feature characters with names like Xaxon and Eldrik, and sport dialogue that's jammed with esoteric code words, arcane phrases and millennial paranoia. These stories may indeed be original, but they're impossible to understand and even more impossible to produce. No studio V.P. in her right mind would touch them.

We also frequently read historical biographies about figures few people have ever heard of, science-fiction opuses that would cost the entire gross national product of Costa Rica to put onscreen, or "true stories" that have relevance only to those people who actually experienced the events portrayed. The people who write these scripts clearly believe in their material, and that's fine. Yet their choice of subject matter (i.e., Uncle Ralph's Alzheimer's) just as clearly shows little sensitivity to the demands of the marketplace.

The same goes for people who try to revive dead genres – westerns, musicals, sword-and-sandal epics, etc. They inevitably fail. When an exception occurs, such as Kevin Williamson's revival of the teen horror genre with the screenplay for *Scream*, it's because the script is itself exceptional, and provides a new twist on conventions. (It also helps if they're cheap to produce.) Studios will sometimes take a leap of faith if it doesn't involve a major financial risk.

So what do buyers want? Well, that changes weekly, depending on what's making money at the box office. And, as we said earlier, it's usually lethal to try to exploit a current trend. Generally speaking, those screenplays that are purchased from new writers tend to fall into three basic categories: thrillers (small casts, lots of suspense, person-to-person violence); action pictures (car chases, things that blow up real good); and comedies (romantic and/or broad). They're what's known as mainstream or commercial movies. They're the kinds of movies mass audiences like to go see, so they're naturally the kinds of stories studios want to buy.

Here are some other guidelines to consider when deciding on a project:

• The story should be "contemporary." Most buyers have a negative knee-jerk reaction when it comes to period pieces. Stories set in other eras are inevitably more expensive to produce than films set in the modern day, and they tend not to do particularly well at the box-office (*Titanic* notwithstanding).

• The story should be castable with *English-speaking actors*. You might have the greatest script ever written about Australian aborigines, but if there isn't a major role for a Tom Cruise or a Julia Roberts or a Jim Carrey, chances are it won't be purchased. *Stars sell movies.* Maybe not to the public, but certainly to studios. And the biggest stars in the biggest movies speak English. Comprende?

• The project should be, in its physical dimensions, small enough to be produced on a reasonable budget. The average studio film today costs approximately $60 million to make and another $60 million to distribute. (And all that will get you is two name stars sitting at a table talking.) If you're an unproduced writer, you're best advised to keep your story's parameters limited, to minimize your buyer's financial exposure. Fight scenes, car chases and explosions are okay – even desirable – but don't write huge disaster epics. Don't write war movies. Don't write anything that involves the proverbial cast of thousands. Concentrate on *character*. Nine times out of ten, a character-driven script garners the attention of actors, agents, producers, directors and studios alike.

• Don't set the story in a "physically hostile location." When Jeff Katzenberg ran Disney's motion picture division in the 1980s, he issued an edict that pithily elucidated his criteria for spec scripts: "No sand, no snow, no water." Knowing the production nightmares that can result from trying to shoot films in even marginally hostile locations, Katzenberg wanted to make sure that the stories he bought were as practical to make as possible. Today, Disney and the other studios may not be *this* strict, but they're still cautious when considering a project set in a demanding or inaccessible location.

We recently read a spec script that violated virtually every one of these rules. It was an historical biography set in World War II-era China. Not only was the story set in the past and in a remote locale, but three-quarters of the cast was Chinese and the premise hinged on a number of expansive (and expensive) battle scenes between the Chinese and Japanese armies. It didn't matter how good the writing was: we felt there was simply no way a studio was going to buy this project from an unknown writer. To date, this analysis has proved correct.

"But wait!" we hear you cry again. "What about films like *Schindler's List*? Or *Dances With Wolves*? Or *Titanic*? These films were big, difficult period pieces that went on to make hundreds of millions of dollars and win loads of Academy Awards. Aren't *these* the kinds of scripts Hollywood wants to buy?"

The answer is Yes. These *are* the kinds of scripts Hollywood wants to buy. Just not from *you*.

These high-risk projects were all written, produced and directed by people who have been in the business long enough – and have created a long enough string of successes – to finally wield the kind of clout necessary to get them made. They were created by people who had enough power to walk into a studio president's office and say, "Give me $100 million to make my movie – or else." They had a "reputation" other people could bank on.

And they didn't earn their reputations overnight. Long before Steven Spielberg could make *Schindler's List*, he had to direct TV shows for Universal and make tight little thrillers like *Duel* and *The Sugarland Express*; not to mention prove his bankability with *Jaws*, *E.T.*, *Jurassic Park*, etc. Before Kevin Costner could make *Dances With Wolves*, he had to act in such mainstream fare as *The Untouchables, No Way Out,* and *Sizzle Beach, USA.* Mel Gibson earned his box-office clout through a series of action films like *The Road Warrior* and the *Lethal Weapon* clones before embarking on *Braveheart.* And James Cameron, of course, cut his teeth on such Roger Corman classics as *Battle Beyond the Stars* and *Galaxy of Terror* before going on to write and direct *The Terminator, Aliens, Terminator 2* and *True Lies.*

No one starts out on top. Least of all you. If you have a personal project you're just dying to do but that is not readily commercial, keep it under wraps until you've accumulated enough credits that a studio *wants* to take a risk with you. Until that time arrives, don't be a putz. Give 'em what they want.

HOLLYWOOD RULE #3: NEVER SECOND-GUESS THE MARKET

There is a flip side to *Hollywood Rule #2*. On one hand, you must give buyers what they want. Hollywood is, and always will be a buyers' market, with supply far outstripping demand. But on the other hand, trying to specifically tailor a product for the marketplace will probably be an exercise in futility. Although we all aim to please, second-guessing rarely works.

The temptation to second-guess is powerful. Extremely powerful. Everyone in Hollywood is looking for the Sure Thing – the Slam Dunk – but since we're always unsure of our own tastes and opinions, our natural instinct is to look at what everyone else is doing and simply follow suit. Like students of Kabbalah meticulously searching the Bible for God's hidden messages, we often find ourselves sifting through *Daily Variety* and *The Hollywood Reporter* for revelations about hot topics or genres that will lead to a fast, easy big-money deal. A broad comedy opened at No. 1 this weekend? Then we'll write a broad comedy! A sci-fi action spec about an alien bounty hunter just sold to Columbia for $750,000? Quick, find sci-fi action specs about alien bounty hunters to produce!

The problem, of course, is that once a trend is identified, *everyone* in town immediately jumps on the same bandwagon, which makes it nearly impossible for any one script to get much attention. And since a feature script can take anywhere from three months to a year to write and even longer to develop, taking your inspiration or cue from the current box-office champ will inevitably put you weeks, if not months, *behind* the curve.

There's only one way to keep from second-guessing the market-place, and that's to develop what you *want* to develop. This is always a good idea because, chiefly, passion has an eerie way of elevating the quality of creative work. Also, if you never see a dime from your labors, at least you'll have gotten some pleasure from the experience.

The caveat here is that, to be a commercial success, your sensibili-ties and those of the marketplace must be in sync. You can't cater to

popular tastes without having those tastes yourself. Movies and television are mass media, and their products only become financially
viable when they appeal to tens of millions of people, both in America
and around the world. If your tastes tend toward the avant-garde and
the esoteric, then Hollywood is probably *not* the place for you. If you
like the odd and offbeat, you're better off pursuing the independent art-
house market than trying to go the studio route.

But assuming your tastes *are* mainstream, how do you choose what
to write, produce or direct? How do you avoid the Second-Guessing
Syndrome (SGS)? Here's a common-sense strategy:

First, identify the types of films and TV shows you actually like to
watch. Do you enjoy big, loud action pictures? Intelligent period
dramas? Slapstick sitcoms? Women-in-jeopardy TV movies? The
type of stories you like best, the kind of films you'll actually go out of
your way to see, are precisely the sort of feature film or TV episode
you should choose to develop.

Although this may seem like an obvious first step, you'd be surprised at how many budding James L. Brooks fail to take it. People
who really enjoy Merchant-Ivory-style period dramas often opt to
write (or attach themselves to direct) romantic comedies or buddy cop
movies because they think that's what sells. Folks who really get off
on juvenile TV shows like *Family Matters* or *Sabrina the Teenage
Witch* will too often attempt to write spec for *ER* or *NYPD Blue* just so
friends and colleagues won't regard them as lowbrows. This is SGS at
its worst, and the results of such cynical attempts are usually mediocre
at best (just like 80% of movies made by Hollywood).

Next, once you've found your genre, make sure you're bringing
something new to the table. What constitutes something new? Well,
it's usually *not* a wholly new plotline or never-before-seen set of character relationships. (Such things probably don't even exist.) No, in
Hollywood, new usually means putting a unique twist on an old story.
This can involve an unusual character, an odd setting, or – as in the
case of *Scream* (1996) – a fresh new attitude.

Finally, you always want to stay ahead of the curve. Fads and trends
usually only get coverage in the mass media at the time they peak; by

that point, they're already on their way out. Remember back in 1990, we got not one, but *two* lambada movies (*Lambada* and *The Forbidden Dance*) a good year after that particular dance craze had already come and gone? A few years later, we got all kinds of movies trying to exploit computers and the Internet (*The Net, Johnny Mnemonic, Hackers*). Most failed to make their money back.

The point is, if a topic is hot, stay away from it – no matter how commercial you think it might be at the moment. If a subject is *that* popular, then chances are everyone in town is trying to exploit it, and you'll never beat the Big Boys at this game. They can move a lot faster than you can. And if, by some fortuitous twist of fate, your faddish movie *does* sell and get made, chances are that public interest will have waned and the eventual product will be a box office bust (See the disco disaster *Can't Stop the Music* – 1980). And that's not going to help your career any.

Ironically, you can stay ahead of the curve by concentrating on themes and topics that are of a timeless, universal nature. High-concept comedies that exploit age-old human fears and foibles, dramas that explore various aspects of human morality, and action/adventure stories that pit good against evil are all viable grist for the Hollywood mill.

Before moving on, we'd like to emphasize the need for *passion* in everything you do. Hollywood is a town driven by emotions, not ideas. Contrary to popular opinion, money is *not* the bottom line. If it were, we'd never have gotten *The Last Emperor, Driving Miss Daisy, Schindler's List, Kundun* or *Titanic* (all of these films were expected to, at best, break even). Although good ideas and highly developed technical skills are helpful; there's nothing that promotes long-term success like an overwhelming belief in the *value* of what you're doing. Passion has helped innumerable filmmakers overcome seemingly insurmountable hurdles. In the late 1960s, the script for *Love Story* was rejected by every studio in town and only produced after tenacious producer Robert Evans managed to secure independent financing. It went on to become one of the top-grossing films of the 1970s. Producer Wendy Finerman had writer Eric Roth's script for *Forrest*

Gump in development for nearly a decade before it finally went on to become a box-office megahit and sweep the 1994 Academy Awards. Writer-producer-director James Cameron forfeited his entire director's salary and back-end participation so that Fox would allow him to make *Titanic* meet his exacting technical standards. The result was eleven Academy Awards (including Best Picture) and almost two billion dollars in worldwide box-office receipts. Success in Hollywood is all about overcoming resistance. And if anyone is going to believe in your work, you have to believe in it first. "Are you saying that the people who create lowbrow comedies, mindless action pictures, and juvenile sitcoms actually have a passion for what they do?" we hear you ask. You bet they do. The people behind movies like *Tommy Boy* and *Dante's Peak,* or TV shows like *That '70s Show* and *Walker, Texas Ranger* really do derive pleasure from the work itself. If they didn't, such things wouldn't get made at all. In his recent autobiography, *Wake Me When It's Funny*, writer-producer-actor Garry Marshall – the man who brought us TV's *Happy Days*, *Laverne & Shirley* and *Mork & Mindy* as well as such feature films as *Pretty Woman* and *Beaches* – openly admits that most of his product has been middlebrow, but makes no apology for it. That's *his* sense of humor. That's what he likes to *watch*. As a writer/director his product reflects his own personal tastes. And enough people share that taste to have made him a millionaire many times over. The fact is, money alone won't put words on paper or develop a project for production. It takes some degree of genuine inspiration. And that many of the products seemingly geared to the lowest common denominator do major box-office or run for years and years on TV demonstrates that their creators are connecting with large numbers of people who have similar sensibilities, however debased. Don't second-guess the market. Write what you *want* to write; produce what you *want* to produce. But only do so after establishing that your personal sensibilities are in sync with the marketplace, and that there's likely to be one or more buyers who will warm to what you have to sell. While passion is critical, to pursue on the basis of passion alone is foolhardy. In the end, you still have to give 'em what they want.

HOLLYWOOD RULE #4: REMEMBER, EVERYTHING OLD IS NEW AGAIN

Now we've talked about bringing something new to the table and staying ahead of the curve. Those unfamiliar with Hollywood often wonder how to do this, since predicting which way public tastes will go is tantamount to trying to divine next week's Lotto numbers.

Here are some industry secrets that should prove helpful.

First, in Hollywood, $1 + 1 = 3$. No, we're not talking about studio accounting practices. We're talking about how a good many studio projects are conceived and sold. You take one familiar movie, combine it with another familiar movie, and the result is a "new" idea that one hopes will be bigger and better than its antecedents.

For instance, *Star Wars* + V = *Independence Day. Ghostbusters* + *E.T.* = *Men in Black. Rain Man* + *Zelig* = *Forrest Gump. Westworld* + *King Kong* = *Jurassic Park. Jaws* + *The African Queen* = *Anaconda.*

In Hollywoodspeak, this type of combination is called The Meet. When coming up with an idea, you say, It's *Con Air* Meets *The Bridges of Madison County*, or its *Tootsie* Meets *The Dirty Dozen.* The Meet is a kind of industry shorthand everyone in town understands, and it's a great way to communicate your ideas quickly and efficiently. (See opening scenes of *The Player.*)

In fact, if you *can't* compare your idea to a previous hit, it could be a problem. As stated earlier, studios like ideas that are "fresh and original," but still in the mainstream. If you say your film is totally new, unlike anything that's ever been done before, executives are bound to get skittish. Hollywood is not famous for taking risks, not with $60-100 million, and not on the word of someone with little or no track record. Even if you have to *force* a comparison – "Well, it's kind of like *Titanic*, but modern-day and without the boat" – it's better than having no reference point at all.

Warning: Don't reference movies that were bombs, or may be so old that the 27-year-old creative executive you're pitching to may not have heard of it. You don't want to say, "It's like *Ishtar* Meets *The Postman* – only good!" or "It's *Call Northside 777* Meets *Miracle in Milan*."

You're apt to be met with nothing but a blank stare. Creative executives are not known for their film literacy – or their attention spans.

(However, there are many old films that, because they're industry benchmarks, you can always reference with assurance. This list includes, but is not limited to, *Citizen Kane, Casablanca, The Wizard of Oz, The African Queen, The Treasure of the Sierra Madre, Sunset Blvd.* and *Chinatown.* An exec may not have seen any of these films, but he'll never admit to it.)

In addition to recombinant concepts, studios like old ideas that have been cleverly repackaged. The seemingly recent flurry of remakes (*Sabrina, Flubber*) and movies based on old TV shows (*Lost in Space, The Addams Family, The Fugitive*) is actually just the continuation of the long Hollywood tradition of putting old wine in new bottles.

Since its inception, the American movie business plundered books, stage plays, and even other movies for their established marquee value. For instance, *A Star is Born* has been made three times; first in 1937 as a drama starring Janet Gaynor and Frederic March, in 1954 as a musical starring Judy Garland and James Mason, and finally in 1976 with Barbra Streisand and Kris Kristofferson. (A new rock version is reportedly in the works.) *The Maltese Falcon* was made twice; in 1931 and 1936, before being remade again by writer/director John Huston in the definitive 1941 version. Even *The Incredible Mr. Limpet* (1964) is about to be remade starring Jim Carrey.

But although Hollywood loves digging up the dead, don't think you can walk into a studio office, say, "Let's remake *Ben-Hur*" and get a deal. (Although this is precisely what actress/producer Cindy Williams did at Disney with *Father of the Bride.*) First, you have to get the "rights" to the underlying material. This can prove difficult, especially if the material is a property the studio already owns.

But it's not impossible. Sometimes older material, books in particular, can be secured by contacting the author, publishing house, or other copyright holder, and stating your intentions. Best-selling author Stephen King granted the rights to one of his short stories (*The Shawshank Redemption*) to a little-known filmmaker Frank Darabont, just because the guy was so damned enthusiastic.

You can also draw "inspiration" from existing material and come up with your own original stories in the same genre. Sometimes, all it takes is a single twist. For example, start with Agatha Christie's classic mystery *And Then There Were None* (1945), that war-horse about ten people trapped on an island who get murdered one by one. Now set it in outer space. Voila! You've got *Alien* (1979). Now take that same story and twist it to make the elusive killer the *hero*, and Poof! You've got *Die Hard* (1988). Finally, take *that* story; make the hero President of the United States, and Ta Da! You've got *Air Force One* (1997).

When drawing inspiration from the past, you should also recognize that trends tend to move in *twenty-year cycles*. People traditionally gravitate toward the types of entertainment they grew up with. When you hit thirty, you long for the movies, music and TV shows you enjoyed when you were ten. And because of the way the human psyche works, it takes two full decades for something to turn from being a novelty to popular to passe to, finally, nostalgic.

For example, in the 1960s, everyone was looking back on World War II with movies like *The Great Escape* and *The Guns of Navarone*, and TV shows like *Hogan's Heroes* and *McHale's Navy*. The 1970s gave us the '50s *redux* with *Happy Days* and *Laverne & Shirley*, and movies like *American Graffiti* and *Grease*. In the 1980s, the '60s become hot again with TV shows like *The Wonder Years* and such movies as *Back to the Beach, The Flamingo Kid, Platoon* and *Full Metal Jacket*. Now, in the late '90s, we're revisiting the '70s and '80s with *Boogie Nights, Donnie Brasco* and *The Wedding Singer* while reviving TV shows like *The Brady Bunch* and the entire teen horror genre. It's no accident that one of the top-grossing hits of 1997 was *Star Wars: The Special Edition*, a technologically tweaked version of a film released *twenty years prior*.

More evidence of the twenty-year cycle can be found in the life of that all-American classic character *Superman*. The Man of Steel was created as a comic book hero in the mid-1930s. Two decades later, he became a television staple. It took another twenty years for the first major *Superman* feature to be made. And now, twenty years since then, a *new* one is in the works.

What's going to be hot in the next few years? One sure way to get ahead of the curve is to look *back* twenty years. As we enter the first decade of the 21st Century, we can look forward to a renewed interest in the people, events, and issues of the 1980s. Determine what kind of entertainment was popular *then*, and put some modern sheen on it. A story need not be set in the 1980s to be a 1980s story. It need only reflect the "sensibilities" of that era. (*Star Wars*, for example, while set in a galaxy far, far away, is still very much a '70s film. The *Mission: Impossible* movie, while set in the present day, reflected the Cold War paranoia of an earlier era.)

Recognize that in Hollywood, everything old is eventually new again. And as much as studios say they like "fresh and original," they find real comfort in the familiar. So do audiences. That's why they keep making *Star Trek* and James Bond movies. Learn how to take an old idea and make it look new – or how to couch a truly new idea in familiar terms – and you'll be someone the studios will want to get to know.

HOLLYWOOD RULE #5: BE DETAIL-ORIENTED

Everyone has a great idea for a movie. Just ask. Actually, you don't even have to ask. Go to a party, mention that you're in the Business, and nine times out of ten someone will pull you aside and say, "You know, I've got a story that's a sure-fire Academy Award-winner. It's about this real estate agent..." Oh, yeah, and the guy will be a real estate agent.

So what's the difference between the bore you meet over cocktail weenies and the writers, directors or producers who go into studios to pitch their projects? If they're amateurs, probably not much beyond the label on their designer jackets. It's not unusual for fledgling filmmakers to enter the lion's den bearing nothing but the germ of an idea and visions of their faces gracing the cover of *Premiere*. As you might imagine, this is about as smart as facing Patton's 3rd Army with nothing but a loincloth and a peashooter. And the results can be just as bloody.

Those who know the *Hollywood Rules* know better. They know that everyone has an idea for a movie, but few have developed that idea sufficiently to turn their idea into a bona fide *story*. To do so requires several key ingredients:

Structure. The process of properly laying out a screen story is complex enough to fill volumes...and it has. We're not going to go into it here. That's why they invented Samuel French's bookstore. If you've followed the guidelines set forth in Chapter Four, you've already read all the books, taken all the classes, attended all the seminars, and read all the screenplays necessary to know how to do this. When you go in to talk about your film project, you'll be able to express it in terms of an Act One (the set-up), an Act Two (escalating conflict), and an Act Three (climax and resolution). You'll never go in with just a premise. At the very least, you'll be able to tell your buyer how your story ends and what the protagonist wants.

Character Arc. Buyers usually want to know how the hero changes over the course of the story. "He goes from being suicidal to embracing life." "She learns to accept love." "He comes to accept his son as an adult." Producers love stories in which people think and behave differently at the end from how they did at the beginning. When buyers ask you "What's the arc?" you not only have to know what they're talking about; you need to give them an intelligent answer.

Theme. This is an area we're constantly hounding would-be filmmakers to put more thought into. Far too many screen stories are really nothing but a series of actions directed toward solving a particular problem: *Two cops pursue a bad guy. A young woman wants to marry the unattainable man. Someone tries to get away with murder.* These stories may work moment-by-moment, but when they're over, we're usually left feeling empty and unsatisfied.

In addition to structure and character arc, you should also be able to talk about your movie in terms of its theme. This theme should be designed around a provocative statement, or a question for which there is no easy answer. For example, *Schindler's List* (1993) wasn't just a recreation of the Holocaust. It dramatically addressed the idea that "He who saves one life saves the world." Its theme-heroism. On a lighter note, the following year's Best Picture winner *Forrest Gump* had an explicit theme of Fate expressed by the oft-quoted line, "Life is like a box of chocolates – you never know what you're going to get." In other words, life is just one damned thing after another.

For a theme to be dramatically viable, one needs to be able to effectively argue either side. A theme such as "Murder is bad" isn't very interesting because you'll find few people who can effectively argue that "Murder is good." On the other hand, *many* people lead their lives on the premise that one man really can make a difference, or that life is just one damned thing after another.

When trying to sell your story, you need to be able to present your theme in a natural, organic way. Perhaps you include it as a snippet of dialogue, or use it as the "moral" or "lesson" your hero learns at the story's conclusion. Whatever route you take, you should know ahead of time what your theme is. If you don't have one, your story will be about nothing. And, since the farewell of *Seinfeld*, the market for "nothing" is thin indeed.

Story Credibility. Here's where details are critical. In their eagerness to make a deal, too many writers, directors and producers fail to take the time necessary to make sure that their stories actually make sense. They don't bother to research their subject matter, or talk to people who might provide them with invaluable insights on the subjects they've chosen to dramatize. As a result, these stories never get sold; if they do, they're not nearly as effective as they otherwise could have been.

As filmmakers, we must recognize that we're in the business of lying. We ask our audiences to believe – even though they know it's all artifice – that what they're seeing on the screen is really happening. ("Willing suspension of disbelief.") As any ad man, used car dealer, lawyer, or politician will tell you, a really good lie is ninety- percent truth. Support a statement with known facts, and your audience will accept the bits you've fabricated. A kernel of truth can "sell" even the wildest of scenarios. For example, *Jurassic Park* wouldn't have been nearly as effective if Michael Crichton and Steven Spielberg hadn't justified their CGI dinosaurs with a bit of hard science about recombinant DNA. *The X-Files* grew from a cult TV show to Top 20 hit and successful feature film based, in large part, on its writers' ability to suggest documented precedents for even the weirdest mutants, monsters, and paranormal phenomena. In their sci-fi classic *2001: A Space Odyssey* (1968), Stanley

Kubrick and Arthur C. Clarke were able to explore the very nature of God Himself by first grounding their story in hard scientific principles (a strategy later copied – but not quite duplicated – in 1997's *Contact*).

Research can also lead to character facets or story twists you might not have otherwise considered. Truth often really is stranger than fiction, and the real world is rife with people, plots, and dramatic ironies that you'll never discover by simply staring at a blank computer screen. For example, much of Dustin Hoffman's memorable portrayal of autistic-savant Raymond Babbitt in *Rain Man* (1988) was based on his spending time with actual people afflicted with autism. (This research also influenced the screenplay's eventual outcome.) The elderly Rose in *Titanic* throws clay pots because writer/director James Cameron met and interviewed 103-year-old sculptor Beatrice Wood while doing background for his historical epic. Matt Damon's amazing mathematical prowess in *Good Will Hunting* (1997) was credible only because he and co-author Ben Affleck took the time to research the real world of advanced mathematics. (You think anyone could make that stuff up?)

Yet despite the obvious value of research, you'd be surprised to discover how many filmmakers concoct their storylines with only the most rudimentary knowledge of their subject matter. They figure, "Hey, if it sells, *then* I'll do the research." Sorry, but it doesn't work that way.

If you're going to develop a medical drama, learn something about medicine. (Michael Crichton got a medical degree before he wrote his first novel, *The Andromeda Strain*.) If you're going to develop a legal thriller, learn something about law. (It's no accident that both best-selling novelist John Grisham and TV's David E. Kelley – *L.A. Law, Ally McBeal* – are ex-lawyers.) Don't write a military drama without some exposure to the military. (Writer Douglas Day Stewart had been through Navy aviator training in the Pacific Northwest before penning the screenplay to 1982's *An Officer and a Gentleman*.) It doesn't matter if you're developing a story about cops, crooks, bricklayers or trapeze artists: know what you write and write what you know.

This holds true even in such fantastical genres as science fiction. It's amazing how many people write, pitch and/or develop sci-fi and techno-thrillers without even the most basic knowledge of science and technology. They have people flying to the moon in space shuttles, doing DNA analyses in seconds, and dodging flaming meteors in the vacuum of space. They figure, "Hey, no one knows about this stuff, so they won't care." But what they're really saying is, "I don't know about this stuff, and I'm too damned lazy to find out." The bottom line is, most of us have at least a high school education; we read newspapers, watch television, and we live in a world of high technology. We may not all be rocket scientists, brain surgeons, trial lawyers or master detectives, but most of us can smell something fishy. As filmmakers, we owe it to our audiences not to insult their collective intelligence.

To reiterate: Frame your movie in terms of structure, character and theme. Then research, research, research. Know what you're talking about. Remember, Knowledge is Power. And in Hollywood, Power is *Everything*.

HOLLYWOOD RULE #6: READ EVERYTHING

Have we mentioned that Knowledge is Power? Being a committed follower of the *Hollywood Rules*, it is your responsibility to spend part of each and every day expanding your power via the accumulation of said knowledge.

What should you spend your time learning about? *Everything*. As a filmmaker, your purview extends beyond the limited confines of Hollywoodland to embrace the entire depth and breadth of human existence. If something's going on in the world, it's your job to know about it...and exploit it.

Begin with the obvious: the Trades. In Hollywood, this means *Daily Variety* and *The Hollywood Reporter*. These daily publications are the express lane on Hollywood's information superhighway. Subscribe to them both. Read them cover to cover. From them, you'll quickly learn what big project just sold to what studio – and for how much. You'll learn what production company just got a big infusion of cash – and so is ready to buy. You'll read which actors and directors have just been attached to which movies – which immediately makes them more valuable if you can attach them to *your* project. You'll learn who the movers and shakers are, and where they are. If one of your contacts lands a big deal or big promotion, it'll be in the trades. Send a card or make a congratulatory phone call (see *Hollywood Rule #10*).

Both *Daily Variety* and *The Hollywood Reporter* publish weekly charts on the top domestic and international grossers for that week. If you see that a romantic comedy has just opened well, be ready to pitch a romantic comedy. If a big-budget science-fiction film just raked in $30 million in its first three days, pray you have a big-budget science-fiction film in your repertoire. On the other hand, if a big-budget science-fiction film has just tanked, grossing just less than *Home Alone 7*, you'll know that this probably isn't a good time to go into a studio brandishing a big-budget science-fiction project. Wait a few weeks. In this town, memories only last until the next batch of grosses are announced.

In addition to facts and figures, *Daily Variety* and *The Hollywood Reporter* feature regular commentaries on topical subjects you'll find to be excellent grist for pitch-meeting conversation. If a columnist has just lamented the sorry state of romantic heroines, mention how you agree or disagree with this assessment when pitching your own romance. If an editorial has just blasted a particular actor, screenwriter, producer, or director, you can talk about how the columnist was dead-on – or express your sympathies for the wounded target. Remember, as a successful follower of *The Hollywood Rules*, the person you're meeting with has no doubt read the same article, which immediately gives you something in common.

Beyond the industry trades, there's a host of other publications you want to keep your eye on. There are the mass-media entertainment magazines like *Premiere* and *Entertainment Weekly*. In addition to in-depth features about films and filmmakers, both these magazines publish annual "100 Most Powerful People in Hollywood" lists, which are good for tracking the perceived rise and fall of the people who'll inevitably need to help further your own career. (And you know you've made it when *you* appear on one of these lists.)

And don't neglect the more specialized entertainment magazines like *American Filmmaker* (published by the American Film Institute),

Filmmaker (independent films), *Film Comment* (analysis and criticism), *Fade In:* (*the* magazine of the entertainment industry; also publishes a useful top 100 list of "People You Need to Know in Hollywood"), and *Cineaste* (the art and politics of film). All of these publications carry news and features you'll inevitably find interesting – if not immediately useful – and they're critical to knowing who's who, what's what, what's hot and what's not in this business we call show.

And while we're looking for hot Hollywood headlines, let's not forget the newest source of late-breaking news, rumors, scandal and just plain B.S.: the Internet. There are so many movie-related websites available that it's impossible to list them all here. However, a few of the best sites you should click up regularly include Mr. Showbiz (mrshowbiz.com), Entertainment News Daily (www.entertainmentnewsdaily.com), Dark Horizons (www.darkhorizons.com), the infamous Ain't It Cool News (www.aint-it-cool-news.com), and AOL's Hollywood Cafe – where you'll meet industry professionals and fellow aspiring filmmakers. And while you're online, take some time to go to a search engine, punch in movie news, and see where it takes you. These days, you never know what juicy tidbits you might find in cyberspace.

Filmmakers spend so much time immersed in illusion; it's easy to forget about the real world. Don't. Reality is where it all begins, even for followers of *The Hollywood Rules*.

Being a denizen of L.A. – and, as we said, you'd better be – you'll naturally want to subscribe to the *Los Angeles Times*. If nothing else, its Calendar entertainment section is one of the best around, featuring articles and commentaries that inevitably become part of pitch-meeting and studio commissary schmoozing.

Other newsstand staples include *Time, Newsweek, People, Us,* and *Vanity Fair*. With these magazines, you're not just looking for Hollywood news but information about real-life events that can jump-start your creativity or perhaps even lead you to acquiring the rights to riveting true-life stories. (Every year, a handful of feature films and hoards of made-for-TV movies are based on real-life stories. Where do you think these filmmakers get their ideas? Their own imaginations?)

Also pillage old novels and plays in the public domain – a great idea can be found anywhere. Once you develop the adaptation, the material can be your ticket inside the studio gates – as the writer, director or producer.

Finally, remember to read scripts. *Lots* of scripts. Find out what's in the market. Learn about what's selling. If you're a writer, study the competition. If you're a producer or director, uncover the hot new talent so you can get them working with you.

If you've already got an agent, said agent can be an excellent source for getting a hold of other people's spec scripts. There are also your other contacts for this.

Of course, no one expects you to read everything. If you're following the *Hollywood Rules*, you probably barely have time to gas your car on your way to your next pitch meeting. Just be sure to subscribe to those publications most critical to your particular field, keep your eyes on the newsstands, and devote at least fifteen minutes a day to perusing the headlines. When you're stuck for an idea, there's nothing more inspiring than the outrageous conduct of your fellow human beings.

HOLLYWOOD RULE #7: BE A PROFESSIONAL, OR AT LEAST LOOK LIKE ONE

Hollywood is a town built on reputation. When you see a forty-year-old action star leap from an airplane without a parachute, your immediate response might be "Whoa, this guy is good." The truth is, the star is actually fifty, that's not him leaping out of the airplane, the guy leaping actually *does* have a parachute, and the whole shot is probably composited on a computer anyway.

Being steeped in this world of artifice, filmmakers can't help but construct carefully orchestrated images for their personal lives as well. This is particularly true of their public personas. From the $100 ties they wear to their jobs in the CAA mailroom, from the leased Porsche Boxsters they turn over to the valets at Mortons to the Harry Winston diamonds they borrow to wear to the Academy Awards, Hollywood professionals are careful to always project an image of success, confidence, strength, and professionalism. By the same token, they're careful to associate only with people who project this same well-honed image.

Now, unless you're already operating in the upper echelons of Movieland, chances are you just don't have the cash necessary to buy a closet full of Armani fashions, a $75,000 sports car, or a house in Bel Air. And plenty of fools go into massive debt attempting to live a movie star's lifestyle while only making a P.A.'s income. (These guys are the classic Hollywood phonies true professionals can spot a mile away.)

But that doesn't mean there aren't easy things you should do – and, more importantly, things you *shouldn't* do – to help create the impression that you're more than just another schmuck out looking to make a deal.

Shallow as it sounds, one of the first things to consider is your choice of mailing address. This address isn't necessarily where you live, only where you have your mail sent. If you already happen to live in West L.A., Santa Monica, Westwood or, bless you, Beverly Hills, Brentwood or Bel Air, this isn't a problem. You already live where professionals are supposed to. There are also many Valley neighborhoods which are more than acceptable, including practically anywhere in the West Valley (Encino, Van Nuys, Woodland Hills, Sherman Oaks), Burbank, Studio City, Glendale and, moving farther east, Pasadena and immediate environments.

Any coastal community from Malibu south to Redondo Beach is fair game, but if it becomes known you live in Long Beach, people are apt to look at you askance. (Its image remains that of a blue-collar city, one known principally for its shipyards.) With quality-of-life issues getting increasingly important and L.A.-bashing now a favorite pastime even among locals, it's becoming more and more acceptable for creative types – especially writers – to live in Orange County. But again, stick with the coastal communities like Huntington Beach, Newport Beach and Laguna Beach. Everyone wants to live in a beach community, even if your apartment happens to be five miles inland.

If you live anywhere else – and this includes Hollywood itself – you should consider renting a post-office box in the choice community nearest you. Have all of your professional correspondence mailed there. (A lot of people still work in Hollywood, but no one in their right mind actually wants to live there – unless it's in the Hills.)

Be very careful about who you reveal your real address to. When throwing parties, only invite your nearest, dearest friends until you can move to a more industry-friendly community. After all, you don't want the right people getting the wrong idea. If you have business cards printed (and unless you're a producer or director *with a production company*, business cards should *not* be a part of your arsenal), make sure the "right" address is listed.

In a town totally dependent on the automobile, your choice of car is also important. (Don't even think about living in Los Angeles without your own wheels. Public transportation here is a joke, and the people who use it are generally not the types you want to get in close physical proximity to.) We'd all like to drive Mercedes, Porsches and Ferraris, but again, not all of us can afford it. But that doesn't mean you can't drive with a little style.

If your auto budget is extremely limited, get creative. Get funky. Driving a 1983 Dodge Colt may make you look like a loser, but a 1963 Studebaker is a conversation piece.

You now know the importance of keeping up with the Business by reading *Variety* and *The Hollywood Reporter*. But if you want to be considered a professional, don't read these trade publications in public. People who go to coffee shops and restaurants to read the trades are invariably wannabes, and everyone knows it. Industry pros subscribe to the trades and have them delivered to their home or office. They don't read them in public. If you want to read something, read a classic novel and show your intellectual side.

The same goes for reading scripts. *Real* producers and directors have scripts covered at the office by professional readers. If you're caught *reading* a screenplay, you yourself will immediately be pegged as a reader – the absolute lowest rung on the development ladder – and not be seen as a person with whom anyone would want to associate.

Writers should also avoid practicing their trade in public. You want to write? Do it at home or at an office. Only losers camp out at Starbucks. And, please, no laptops. They're a sure sign of a person who has absolutely nothing to offer anyone.

Note that the above rules are only valid within the confines of Los Angeles. If you live in Torrance, it's perfectly acceptable to read *The Hollywood Reporter* while sitting at Diedrichs pecking away at your Toshiba Satellite. No one of any importance is going to see you anyway, so go for broke.

Another wannabe faux pas: placing adverts in trade publications advertising yourself and your projects. Unless you enjoy being the brunt of everyone's joke, this is the fastest way to kill an already non-existent career.

Finally, let's talk about attire. While outsiders may look at Hollywood fashion and figure Anything Goes, nothing could be farther from the truth. There *are* uniforms here, but they tend to be segregated by profession and change on an annual basis. (Seasons are not as important here as elsewhere since, in Southern California, there *are* no seasons except for Hot and Wet.) Producers dress differently from directors, who in turn dress differently from writers. And they all dress differently from studio executives ("suits").

The best way to know how *you* should dress is to see how your *competition* is dressing. Try to blend in. You never want to be mistaken for something you're not.

For example, one screenwriter we know – having just recently transplanted himself from the Midwest – arrived at his first big studio meeting dressed in a three-piece suit. To the outside world, that was the standard uniform of anyone going to a business meeting. However, upon his arrival, he was immediately mistaken for a studio executive and undoubtedly laughed at upon his exit from the exec's office. After that, he had a hard time convincing anyone that he actually had an original or creative idea in his head. It wasn't until he learned to dress in jeans, a long-sleeved cotton shirt, running shoes, and a team jacket that people began to actually treat him like a writer.

As a creative type, you should always wear one – and often only one – expensive piece of clothing to a studio meeting. For example, jeans, a black t-shirt, black Converse sneakers and a $500 blazer are a classic male filmmaker's ensemble. And black is the color of choice in Hollywood, so make sure you own lots of it.

If you're working your way up the studio or agency ranks – even from the mailroom – designer suits are your choice of apparel.

Of course, none of this artifice is any substitute for talent. But no one's going to discover your talent if your image repels or confuses them. As with your choice of screen projects, you have to give them what they want. Your image and behavior needs to conform to the dictates of the marketplace. It's an axiom that holds true for most Hollywood professionals throughout their entire careers.

HOLLYWOOD RULE #8: DON'T GO IT ALONE

By now, you've become a True Believer in the Hollywood Rules. Based on your talents and sensibilities, you've chosen a practical career path, found an exciting, commercially viable screen or TV project, and worked your story into a presentable pitch or screenplay. Now it's time to take it to market.

The first thing you'll discover is that you can't do it alone. You're going to need help – professional help – one or more allies who have already established themselves within the Industry, to put you and your work on the Hollywood map.

Why the need for outside expertise? Well, by nature, Hollywood is and always has been a closed shop. It's distrustful of outsiders. With everyone and his mother wanting to be in the movies, producers and studios can't entertain every story idea that comes along. There just isn't time.

So the Industry has constructed a series of barriers – filters, actually – designed to protect its privileged denizens from the seemingly endless flood of mediocrity that pours into the Los Angeles Basin. Having one or more people already on the inside can help you breach these barriers.

How many players do you need on your team? That depends on your professional needs and the moniker you're pursuing. Producers need a wide array of contacts – from D-boys and girls to studio heads to agents, actors, writers and directors – in order to package and shop their material. Generally speaking, there are three types of allies from which to choose if your eye is on writing or directing: the Agent, the Manager, and the Entertainment Lawyer. A team of experts who can put you and your work on the map. You're free to mix and match these people depending on your goals and financial means.

Agents are the grunts; the foot soldiers who every day slog through the muddy trenches of Hollywood to battle the specters of obscurity and unemployment. The difference between an agent and an infantryman is that agents dress better and make a lot more money...sometimes. Agents are often characterized as parasites, vermin, pond scum. But, like bacteria that live in the darkest reaches of our intestines, we'd die without them.

An agent's job is three-tiered. First, they are responsible for knowing *everything* that's happening in the Business. They need to know what's selling and who's buying. They need to know where the assignments are, and who's looking for what. Second, it's the agent's job to represent *you*, the client, to the people who can make a deal. This can only be done efficiently if the agent has already established a relationship and rapport with the prospective buyers, and if those prospective buyers *trust* the agent enough to take his or her word that looking at your project is worth their time. Finally, if the buyer wants to buy, it's up to the agent to negotiate the main points of your contract, such as how much money you get, and when.

In Hollywood, talent rules. Since agents control talent, they've become some of the most influential people in the Industry. It's no coincidence that when Michael Ovitz ran the town's then-number-one talent agency, Creative Artists Agency (CAA), he was universally regarded as The Most Powerful Man in Hollywood.

Agents come in all shapes and sizes. Some work for huge, powerful agencies like the aforementioned CAA, International Creative Management (ICM) or the William Morris Agency. These agencies often represent hundreds of actors, writers, producers and directors, and are experts at packaging entire movies. Other agents work for medium-sized organizations like Endeavor, Paradigm or Gersh. These companies tend to be a bit more specialized than the mondo-agencies, but their power and influence is still considerable. And then there are the dozens of small, "boutique" agencies that may employ only two or three agents, and whose client list is relatively limited.

So how do you decide which is best for you? Well, each type of agency has its advantages and disadvantages. The big agencies tend to primarily represent *big* clients, and these megastars are the focus of most of their activity. While first-time or little-known writers, producers and directors may be taken on as clients at places like CAA and ICM, it's very easy to get lost in the shuffle, to be considered third- or fourth-string in any packaging arrangement; even, perhaps, only to be considered a "hip pocket" client (talent they may believe in but that hasn't *paid off* yet, and is not yet a "real" client). Finally, being a client at a big agency will give you a certain degree of prestige, but it's no guarantee you'll actually get work.

Medium agencies lack the clout of the Big Boys, but they compensate by being able to give their lesser clients more personal attention. Of course, this is all relative. The mid-sized agencies still represent plenty of big clients, and as with CAA, ICM and William Morris, the client who's making money is the one who'll get the lion's share of the agent's attention.

Small and boutique agencies tend to carry only a select list of clients, and there's a better chance that your agent will actually return your phone call *that day* than if you're at a larger organization. The downside is, the small agencies don't have the clout or the resources you may need to get your material to the people who *need* to see it. And they often aren't privy to the inside information at studios concerning upcoming work assignments.

Wherever you may go, agents are *by law* allowed to take no more than ten percent of whatever payments you receive as a result of their efforts.

Regardless of their agency's size, agents can be critical to launching the careers of many Hollywood professionals – but not all of them. Most writers will find agents to be extremely helpful, especially in obtaining writing assignments. They can also get spec material to more buyers than you could on your own. Producers, however, usually have no need for personal agents, but they do need to *know* agents. *Lots* of agents. Agents are their pipeline to new material, material they can then take to studios in hopes of setting up a deal. Directors are caught in the middle. Like producers, directors need fresh, quality material, and agents serve as effective go-betweens in this regard. And, as with writers, agents can help directors find open assignments as well as help in the negotiating of fees and other contract specifics.

So, how do you get an agent to represent you? If you're a writer, the first thing you must have is one or more screenplays they believe they can sell. This is not the same thing as having a well-written script. An agent may respect or even enjoy your writing, but unless she thinks the material is actually *commercial*, she may not be willing to sign you on as a client. (The purely mercenary attitude of agents is legendary.)

Next, it helps substantially if a producer, director, actor, assistant, executive, or fellow writer who the agent already knows can refer you. Most top agents won't even look at unsolicited material, preferring instead to rely on recommendations from people they already know and trust.

If you don't know anyone in the business – or know anyone who knows anyone – then you can always use a query letter to try and spark an agent's attention. First, obtain *The Annual Agency Guide* (available through The Writers Store and Samuel French Bookstores). The guide gives you the names, addresses, phone and fax numbers, genre and submission requirements of both WGA-signatory (those who have formally agreed to follow the Guild's guidelines and standards) and non-WGA-signatory agents, managers and entertainment lawyers. Even if an agency indicates that it accepts unsolicited scripts, don't just send your screenplay. First, mail a *query letter* to see if they're truly interested in your premise. This letter should be short – no more than a page – cordial, concise, and should contain a *brief* (one-paragraph) description of your professional qualifications, if any. In this letter, do *not* blather on about how great you and your friends think your script is, or about how desperate you are to break into the movie business. This will only make you look like an amateur. Instead, be matter-of-fact, putting your primary emphasis on your characters and your story and the elements that make them unusual, if not unique. Which means get straight to the point; no hyperbole or hard sell. Avoid desperate phrases such as, "I guarantee this script will sell for $1 million!" "Steven Spielberg is going to want to do this!" or "I want to get into the movies so much, I'm willing to give this one away for free!" Just give agents what they *really* want to hear – a good story.

Another way to identify agents to contact is by scanning *Variety* and *The Hollywood Reporter* for stories on recent sales. Such stories will always list the agent who negotiated the deal. If you've got an action script, and a particular agent just closed a big action script deal, then chances are this agent is good with action writers. It's an ideal place to start.

If you're a director, you don't need a spec script. What you do need is a reel – a collection of clips, usually on videotape – from shorts or spec videos or spec commercials you've already shot that effectively showcase your talent. For directors just starting out in the Business, this usually means including clips from any student films you may have directed. Reels should include strong *dramatic* or *comedic* moments between actors as well as demonstrations of fancy effects, stunts, and camerawork. Your reel should be professionally assembled, and be anywhere from ten to twenty minutes in length.

To acquire a list of potential director's agents, contact the Director's Guild of America (DGA) and get their list of signatory agents. Write a query letter explaining that you are a new director seeking professional representation, and ask the agent if he/she would like to see your reel. List the productions included on the reel, and when they were filmed.

In the case of both writers and directors, query letters *can* be sent to those agencies that indicate they don't accept unsolicited material. After all, you're just sending a query letter. The worst thing they can do is say "No" – or not respond. But if they *do* respond positively, then that counts as a "solicitation," and you're in the front door. (You also may want to consider that there are certain times of the year when agents are at their busiest, and may not have time to address, or even read, your inquiry. Those periods are: TV-staffing season (January-May) and those months heavy with spec-sales and studio writing assignments (January-May, and September-November).

After you've sent a prospective agent your spec script or demo reel, it may take him/her at least a few weeks to respond. Agents have a *lot* of material from their own clients to sift through on a daily basis. Give the agent at least a month to respond before making a follow-up call. The best time to call agents is usually between the hours of 4:00 PM and 7:00 PM, Tuesdays through Fridays. Never call on a Monday; they're inevitably too busy to talk to *anybody*. Whatever you do, don't make more than one follow-up call every two weeks, and always be cordial and upbeat. Be particularly nice to their assistants. Learn their names, and always talk to them personally before asking to speak to the agent. Assistants like to be acknowledged, and can wield enormous power when it comes to making positive contacts with higher-ups.

Producers have other options when it comes to meeting agents. The most common is to meet agents through social contacts. But there's nothing wrong with calling up an agent, introducing yourself, and inviting the agent out to lunch – although it's always better to drop someone's name with whom they're familiar.

"Hi, I'm Barry Bigshot. I'm a producer looking for low-budget thrillers – projects in the three- to four-million-dollar range. Larry Bigshot said you're someone I should get to know. So, I'd like to set up a lunch."

What self-respecting agent is going to turn down a producer who might buy a client's project – not to mention a free lunch?

When choosing agents, it's critical that you like them and that they like you. A good agent is more than just a business representative; there's a special personal relationship that develops that's part friend, part lover and part father confessor. A bad client-agent relationship is like a bad marriage; everybody wants out, and it's the child – the work – that usually suffers most.

On the other hand, managers can also function like agents: they find work, they provide introductions, and they put scripts on the market. They make deals. But managers serve an extra function; they're advisors who, if skilled, will be able to map your entire career path and be able to make it all happen. Some even have the wherewithal to function as script editors and story consultants.

Very often, it's the manager who sets the client up with an agent. The manager can also recommend the entertainment lawyer when it comes time to nail down a contract. These days, it's not uncommon for managers to also be producers, and thus create the very venues through which their clients acquire employment.

As close as the ideal client-agent relationship is, the client-manager relationship is even closer. Many writers, producers and directors change agents on a regular basis, but keep the same manager for decades. Client-manager relationships have been known to outlast many Hollywood marriages. (But then, so have many four-course dinners.)

Unregulated by law, managers usually charge between ten and fifteen percent for their services. If you're new in this business, you may require both an agent and a manager. The more professional people you surround yourself with, especially those who will work on your behalf and get your name out there, the better.

Many managers are listed in *The Annual Agency Guide*. Other companies and managers can be found in various trade articles about spec sales.

The method for contacting managers is much like that for contacting agents. Begin with any personal references you can exploit. If you know someone who already has a manager, start there. Beyond that, send a query letter just like the one you'd send to an agent. But be sure to indicate that you're looking for *long-term* representation; not just help with a single project.

Even if you do have an agent and/or manager, when it comes time to actually close a deal, you're going to need an entertainment lawyer. An agent or manager can help negotiate a contract in broad terms, but it takes an experienced attorney to go head-to-head with the studio shysters and pound out the brass tacks – like residual schedules and definitions for things like net profits.

Most writers, producers and directors only go to their attorneys when it comes time to actually make a deal – or sue someone. However, some people eschew agents and managers altogether, and rely solely on their lawyers for professional representation. This is not as awkward as it sounds. Most entertainment lawyers are just as plugged-in to the studio scuttlebutt as agents and managers are. They know people, or know people who know people, and can start you on the roundelay of introductions that can eventually lead to a deal. A big difference between lawyers and agents/managers is that the search for client employment is usually only a small part of an attorney's daily activities. Most of an attorney's time is spent negotiating contracts, sending threatening letters, and doing all the other arcane voodoo that lawyers do. Also, while an entertainment lawyer may be able to help get a project into the market via his personal connections, he or she will probably have little knowledge of open writing and directing assignments at the studios. For that, you really do need an agent.

If you're a producer, a good entertainment lawyer is essential to helping you set up studio deals, negotiate with talent, and making sure your interests are looked after. A young producer without a strong, savvy attorney is likely to end up selling star maps on Sunset Boulevard.

Most entertainment lawyers work in one of two ways. Either they take a cut of your income – anywhere from five to ten percent – or they simply charge you on an hourly basis. Often, you have the option to choose which payment method you prefer. If your deal comes together quickly, the hourly rate can be very economical. But since most Hollywood deals *don't* come together quickly – and since lawyers have a nasty habit of billing for every minute they even *think* about you – forking over the ten percent can sometimes be the better deal.

As with agents and managers, a good personal referral is the best way to find an entertainment lawyer. Otherwise, the Yellow Pages is not a bad place to start. You might also check the trades for stories about recent deals – attorneys are often cited in such articles.

"But why do we need anybody at all?" you ask. "I have a great script, and/or an amazing reel. Can't I just send it over to a studio?"

Unfortunately...NO! As noted before, Hollywood is a *closed shop*. Big-time producers and studio honchos see themselves as noblemen ensconced in high-walled castles, while thousands of torch-bearing peasants pound at the gates demanding a three-picture deal and a spread in Brentwood.

Like a civilian trying to get into the inner circle of *La Cosa Nostra*, you need a made man to vouch for you – to put his or her *own* reputation on the line in defense of your talent – in order to do this. An established agent, manager or entertainment lawyer is the equivalent of a made man, a guy the *capo* can trust. Of course, if one of these made men vouches for a talentless loser, he ends up losing credibility and people stop returning his phone calls – the Hollywood equivalent of sleeping with the fishes. So made men tend to be very picky about who they take on.

An exception to this rule involves getting spec material or demo reels directly to stars and smaller-time producers. As always, personal connections can help you clear practically any obstacle the Industry puts in your way. If you know a name actor, or someone at a production company, there's nothing that says you can't slip something to them friend-to-friend. Likewise, a small producer, like agents and managers, may be open to a query letter. Small producers are *always* looking for good material that they can then take to *big* producers. You may have just what they need.

Names and addresses of *all* producers, big and small, can be found in the *Hollywood Creative Directory*. Published quarterly, this book can be purchased, as can *The Annual Agency Guide*, at most Hollywood-area bookstores, or via subscription. The companies and players in the *Directory* change constantly, so make sure you have a current edition. Avoid big producers or those with studio "housekeeping" deals: most of these producers can only be approached through legitimate agents and managers. But this still leaves dozens – if not hundreds – of smaller production companies that *are* fair game. Each listing will usually include several recent features the company has produced; you can use this to determine if they're the kind of producers who'd be interested in your project. For example, a producer who lists two or three low-budget teen comedies probably wouldn't be too responsive to an action/adventure buddy flick.

One critical thing to remember is that neither an agent, manager, nor an attorney – or anyone else of significant stature you come across – can get you work. Only *you* can do that. Even the best agent in Hollywood can't sell a really bad script or get you a housekeeping deal at Sony if your project sucks. The agent, manager and entertainment lawyer are your supporting troops, but *you* are the general. When the battle is joined, it is you and you alone who must do or die.

Now that you realize the power of personal connections, let's explore how you make these connections – especially if you're new to the Hollywood scene...

HOLLYWOOD RULE #9: MAKE THE RIGHT FRIENDS

No doubt you've heard the old adage: "It's not *what* you know, but *who* you know." Well, nowhere is that axiom more relevant than in Hollywood. This is a town driven by connections, contacts, and personal relationships. Knowing the right people can lead you to getting an agent, manager or entertainment lawyer. It can also lead to meeting producers, directors and movie stars which, ultimately, can lead to three-picture deals, an office on the studio lot, and invitations to some real cool parties.

So how do you make these right connections? If you've lived in Southern California for any amount of time, chances are you already know *somebody* in The Business. After all, entertainment is Los Angeles's (not to mention America's) number-one export, employing hundreds of thousands of people. Your initial acquaintance may not be a studio head or an A-list action star, but maybe she's a secretary at a small production company. Or he's an assistant sound editor. Or the gal who cuts Christian Slater's hair. Or the guy who drives the catering truck for *Baywatch*. Or maybe the cousin of the guy who drives the catering truck for *Baywatch*. Whoever it is, *that's your in*!

Someone on the fringe of show business may not seem like much of a connection, but you've heard about the fabled Six Degrees of Separation? (Supposedly you can connect any person to any other person on Earth through no more than six interpersonal relationships.) In Hollywood, you're only *one* person away from someone you need to know. Just ask Kevin Bacon.

Usually, you begin this professional daisy-chain by simply telling your first set of friends about your aspirations, or your specific project, then asking them if they happen to know an industry professional who might be interested in seeing your work. If the answer is "Gee, I'd like to help, but I really don't know anyone like that," take it to the next step. Ask them if they know anyone else in the Business who might be able to steer you on the right path. You can be vague. Any connection is potentially valuable – since it can theoretically lead to dozens of others.

Now, at this point, your initial contacts may get a bit skittish. This is perfectly understandable. Remember that this town is built on reputations, and if they introduce you to people and your project stinks, it's going to reflect badly on *them*. So here you have to take a gamble: you must actually *show* these people what you've got. You must *impress* them. Get them excited about what you're doing. Everyone in town loves to be in a position to later say, "Hey, I *discovered* this star/writer/director" – so give your friends something they can run with.

If these people like your stuff, chances are they will be more than happy to introduce you to their contacts, at which point you start the whole process over again. Finally, somewhere along the line, you'll be referred to the person you *really* want to meet. At that point, if the agent, producer or movie star likes what he/she sees, you're in the game for real.

A word about making friends with movie stars: getting chummy with name actors or actresses can be a great career move, but it's a risky one. Your talent must be strong enough that you can do something for *them*. You can't just be a professional glommer. Stars know when they're being used. And they can get paranoid. When developing a project with a star, make sure everything is *their* idea...they like that.

But what if you're not local? What if you've just come into town (*Hollywood Rule #1*) and you don't know a soul? Fear not. There are plenty of places to make that all-important first contact.

First, you can *buy* yourself a contact. As we already discussed in Chapter Four, you can take courses in your chosen field either through local schools and colleges, or via many of the professional filmmaker seminars you see regularly advertised in *L.A. Weekly, Daily Variety* and *The Hollywood Reporter*.

If you write a strong script or produce an impressive short film, chances are your professor or instructor will be happy to refer you to someone he knows who can further your career. If your professor or instructor doesn't know at least half a dozen good agents or managers, you should seriously question what the hell he/she is doing teaching a course about filmmaking. And demand your money back.

Another way to buy your way in is to join a professional organization. Hollywood is full of them. There's Women in Film and the Hollywood TV and Radio Society. There are social/professional organizations like Chicagoans In the Industry (CITI), Independent Film Project (IFP), and the British Academy of Film and Television Arts (BAFTA). Most only require a few bucks to join, and many hold regular meetings where you can make nice with industry professionals.

You can also attend some of the larger film festivals – Sundance, Toronto Film Festival, Telluride Film Festival – here and elsewhere around the country. For the price of a movie ticket and, if from out of town, a hotel room, you can rub elbows with some of Hollywood's familiar names and faces. If your own face becomes recognizable, you'll find it easy to strike up conversations. And everybody likes to talk in movie lines.

While attending festivals, smile a lot. Be happy. Happy people like to talk to other happy people. But don't force it. No one likes a phony.

If you can't buy yourself a Hollywood contact, you always have the option of begging. Many production companies take on full-time – and part-time – interns who provide their services for nothing except the experience they gain, which in the long run can be invaluable. Being an intern means gaining the trust of people who can help further your career. You'd be surprised how, even as a lowly intern, you'll quickly start getting hit on by other outsiders asking you to help make contacts for *them*!

Some people have gotten intern positions simply by walking into a studio's employment office and saying, "I'm willing to work for free. I'll take whatever you have." Or you can buy a copy of the *Hollywood Creative Directory* and send your resume, along with a letter of inquiry, to every damned listing in the book. And don't forget the talent agencies themselves. There's no better way to get an agent than to bring one coffee every morning, and then, one-day, slip 'em a dynamite screenplay or reel. But *make sure it's dynamite.*

If you take the intern route, prepare to work your butt off. You'll come in early and leave late. You'll do whatever is asked of you – and more – and do it with a smile. Remember, as an intern, your goal is not to become rich and famous, but to *make friends.* You'll get people to help you by first helping *them.*

Now, if all of this groveling seems a bit ignoble to you, just remember that – despite what you may read about USC graduates making $750,000 on their first screenplay or some 21-year-old director making a three-picture deal based on a film he shot in Dayton for $30,000 on maxed-out credit cards – practically no one in this business starts out on top. Like the Harvard MBAs who have to toil in the talent agency mailrooms before being graduated to positions of responsibility, writers, producers and directors often have to content themselves with positions they consider below their station before getting an opportunity to hit the big time. Ironically, it's often these menial positions that give rise to the very opportunities they're seeking...and the humility to appreciate them.

A word to the antisocial: It's not essential to be a social butterfly to make it in Hollywood, although it does help tremendously. Misanthropes *do* manage to have careers in this town – usually as writers. You just have to work hard, especially in the initial stages, when you're seeking someone willing to take you on.

Even if you spend most of your time in a sealed room, after a while you'll meet enough people that you'll be invited to parties. *Go.* Be charming. Drink in moderation. Leave the heavy drugs to the actors. Talk shop. When possible, exchange phone numbers. You never know – the guy you meet over hors d'oeuvres could be your New Best Friend.

Of course, just making contacts isn't enough to build and maintain a Hollywood career. You need to keep those contacts alive and productive.

HOLLYWOOD RULE #10: KEEP IN TOUCH

Like a marriage, maintaining professional contacts takes *work*. In marriage, complacency often leads to divorce. In show business, it often leads to being *forgotten*, which is infinitely worse.

Keep all your contacts, big and small, on your Rolodex. Try to stay in touch with everyone you've met on a regular basis (more importantly, keep them interested in your work). If it's a close relationship, a call every two or three weeks should keep you safely in the loop. If the relationship is more distant, you should still call about once every three months just to remind him/her that you're still alive and active. But note: you need a *reason* to call – something that will be of interest, or help them in some way.

A good way to do this is to keep your eyes on the trades, especially for articles about recent deals in which your contacts are mentioned. As soon as you see a story that features someone you know, give him/her a call to offer your congratulations. Stroke their egos. Tell them about how much you're looking forward to seeing their finished project on screen. But make the call short, two to three minutes tops – unless the person you've called keeps the conversation going. Remember that there are probably dozens of other people waiting in line to make the same call; kiss the same ass.

If a friend or contact gets promoted, send something. A simple congratulatory card will usually suffice. Cards are unobtrusive, and they tend to be kept on desks for a while, thus serving as a constant reminder of your undying respect, admiration and loyalty.

If you're truly good friends with the recent promotee, you can risk going a little bigger. Maybe send a small gift that has some personal meaning between the two of you.

Take advantage of the human need to ingest. The casual meal is the perfect venue to talk shop and pitch projects – many Hollywood types spend more time in restaurants than they do at the office. You can invite your friend out to an early breakfast, late breakfast, early lunch, late lunch, after-hours drink or, if the relationship is strong enough and the person has no domestic responsibilities, dinner. Offer to pick up the tab.

Nobody turns down a free meal.

Be prepared to do favors. In fact, relish such opportunities. If someone asks you to read and comment on their script, do so without hesitation. If someone asks *you* for help finding an entertainment lawyer or meeting a producer, do everything you can to accommodate him/her. *Favors are debts*, and the more debts you can accumulate, the easier it will be to get help when you really need it.

We've discovered the need to go to as many parties as you can arrange to be invited to. Assuming your social calendar isn't packed solid, you can also *throw* the occasional party of your own. It doesn't have to be anything fancy: just beer and munchies and some good music. Invite all your friends – and ask them to bring *their* friends. You've instantly widened your circle of contacts.

Hollywood, being what it is, offers plenty of opportunities to throw parties around a particular theme. We're particularly fond of parties arranged around televised awards shows. For example, every spring, everyone in town who isn't going to the Academy Awards goes to somebody's Oscar party. There are so many of them that many people are obligated to attend several. Fortunately – since the telecast usually runs well over three hours – there's time for one person to make appearances at nearly a half-dozen such events.

In addition to the Oscars, there's the Golden Globes (held in January), the Emmys (held in early September), and scores of others – all of which provide an excuse for you to spin that Rolodex and schmooze.

The great thing about an awards-oriented party is that it's the perfect opportunity for industry people to talk shop in a social atmosphere. Everyone's going to have his or her predictions, favorites and opinions. You'll have no problem breaking the ice, even with total strangers.

HOLLYWOOD RULE #11: DON'T BE A PEST

It's said that patience is a virtue. In Hollywood – a town of microscopic attention spans – it's more than that. It's essential, as essential as a car, a cell phone, and a steady source of caffeine. Not only do most filmmakers have to wait forever for their chance to become an overnight success, but also once the production machinery kicks in, the inactivity can seem almost interminable. "Hurry up and wait" is the unofficial motto of the entire entertainment industry.

When will your patience be tested in Hollywood? Try each and every day. Here's a typical scenario: You have a new screenplay in hand. If you're a writer or director, you'll first want your agent to read it. This takes time. Agents are busy people – usually working on *other* people's careers. So you wait. Perhaps you spend the time anticipating a negative response, mentally preparing a list of reasons why your agent is full of shit. But, lo and behold, your agent responds positively. Now time must pass while he/she puts together a list of prospects. So you wait some more. Now you're probably imagining Steven Spielberg or Richard Donner falling in love with the project and wanting to take you under his wing. Finally, the screenplay goes into the market. You know how you always read in the trades about such-and-such script selling for $2 million after a twelve-hour bidding war that began two minutes after the script hit the streets? Think this will happen to you? Think again. It's going to take days to get your first response, maybe even weeks. So you wait...and wait...and wait some more. You promised yourself you wouldn't even think about money, but it's unavoidable. In your mind, that big fat paycheck is already in the bank. Then, thank God, one or two producers actually *like* the project, and they agree to take it into their respective studios. More waiting. Agonizing waiting. By now, the money you imagined putting in the bank has already been spent on a new car, a new house, and a trip to Paris. Finally, you have a deal. Think your check's going straight into the mail? Dream on. Now your contract has to be *negotiated*. Your contract will be batted about like a badminton shuttlecock for weeks as the various attorneys nit-pick the document to death, arguing about minutiae so trivial you couldn't see it with an electron microscope. At this point, all the excitement and exhilaration that accompanied that phone call from Business Affairs has dissipated and been replaced by the desire to *just get this agony over with!* Now you don't care *how* much money you make, *you just want a friggin' contract!*

Finally – just before you're on your deathbed with the padre reading you last rites – the deal is sealed and you'll get your first payment. Once your agent has taken *his* commission. And wouldn't you know it, that takes time!

At long last, you're ready to roll up your sleeves and get to work. And this involves waiting for notes, waiting for reactions to rewrites, waiting to hear if you're still on the film, waiting to finally get the "greenlight" for production, waiting for stars to say yea or nay, waiting through pre-production, waiting on the set while the cinematographer takes three hours to light a three-second shot, waiting through editing, scoring, and the rest of postproduction, waiting for the damned film to finally be released (on a date that won't get moved), and then that *really* awful wait for the reviews and the first weekend's box-office report.

Did we mention that it helps to be patient in this business?

Of course, many people find it impossible to just sit back and let events take their natural course. They have the gloriously naive belief that they – even in their capacity as a tiny cog in an otherwise unfathomably vast media machine – actually have the power to speed things along. They think that if they call people at least once a day and ask, "So what's happening? Any news? Anything I can do?" they can get a buyer to buy, a star to commit, or a studio to greenlight.

There are many words to describe such people: Eager, Anxious, Excited, Impatient. But mostly, they're just called "pests."

And no one likes to work with a pest.

The classic "Don't call us, we'll call you" didn't arise out of nowhere. People in decision-making positions are not only loath to respond to unsolicited communications, they actually *resent* such intrusions. This is especially true when they themselves are as in the dark about the status of things as you are. Nobody likes to be reminded of his or her own impotence.

To maintain the best possible relations with those people you're working with, only call them when you absolutely must – or if you have a valid pretense. For example, as discussed in *Hollywood Rule #10*, you can always call to discuss a story you saw in the newspaper or read in the trades. Did you just see a great new movie? That's worth calling about. Or you can call to invite an associate out to lunch. But, for God's sake, don't bother your agent with, "So, did we get any offers?" or a studio with, "So, are we getting the greenlight or not?" Believe us, when there's news to report your phone will ring.

Of course, this is all easier said than done. There's nothing more painful than the act of sitting around and waiting. So here's our suggestion: *Don't*. The best cure for the Waitin' Around Blues is *work*. Are you a writer who just finished a screenplay and who's waiting to hear back from prospective producers? Don't wait. Start working on your *next* script. If this one doesn't sell, you're going to want to get a new one into the market as soon as possible anyway. Are you a director waiting to hear if your project is going to be greenlit? Assume that it is and start storyboarding. Or read new scripts in search of your *next* project. The same goes for producers. You can never have too many projects in the pipeline. Inactivity doesn't just promote stagnation; it can actually cause you to *lose* ground by allowing great new projects to escape your attention.

Of course, many people can't work *all* the time. And when you're waiting, time is all you have. So what else can you do with it?

Well, you're a filmmaker, right? Go to movies. The tickets are tax-deductible. Even more radical: read books. And newspapers. And magazines. *The Hollywood Rules* say you're supposed to read everything, right? Here's the time to do it. Have you got a family? Spend time with them. If your project sells, this may be the last time you see them for months.

Or maybe you should just lie around the house downing six-packs and watching *Jerry Springer*. Hey, whatever your style dictates. Just don't keep calling people hoping to get good news. Such overt anxiety communicates insecurity, immaturity, and a total lack of "cool." And this, subliminally or otherwise, can make you look like a loser. And such images have the uncanny knack of becoming self-fulfilling.

Instead, as soon as a project leaves your hands, imagine you've succeeded. Carry yourself as if you've already won that Academy Award. In fact, imagine that you're *so* hot that you can't even be bothered to pick up the phone except to take important incoming calls. Imagine how you'll enjoy your newfound success. Picture the great new house, the shiny new car and the great new clothes.

But please: don't actually buy anything until the check clears the bank.

HOLLYWOOD RULE #12: ALWAYS END THE PHONE CONVERSATION FIRST

The telephone is the instrument that holds all of Hollywood together. It's safe to say that most agents and producers spend more time on the telephone than they do in their cars – and in Southern California, people spend a good third of their lives in their cars. Even writers and directors are likely to spend more time communicating with their underlings and collaborators via Ma Bell than by actual face-to-face contact. It's therefore crucial to master the instrument that is the telephone, and learn to use it to your maximum advantage.

In *Hollywood Rule #10*, we told you how important it is to maintain regular contact with people who can help further your career. (Conversely, in *Hollywood Rule #11*, we advised you to keep such contacts down to tolerable levels.) Now we add one more critical trick to your arsenal of telephone manners: always be the one to end the phone call.

Being the one to terminate the conversation has numerous advantages. First, it puts *you* in a position of power. Since you're the one who's controlling the conversation, you're exercising authority over the guy on the other end – even if the guy on the other end happens to be Rupert Murdoch. Second, you're subtly communicating that you're a busy person; someone to whom time is a valuable commodity. In Hollywood, busy means successful, and everyone wants to do business with someone who's successful. Finally, like a good comedian, you're leaving your audience wanting more. When they want more, they come back. You're therefore laying the foundation for future communications – and future business.

As with everything else in Hollywood, there's an art to ending a phone call. You don't want to slam down the handset in the middle of an important exchange just to be the first one to do so. This isn't a race. Likewise, you can't just say, "I guess that's it. Ciao, baby!" and blow the caller off. No, you have to be polite, gracious...yet have just the right edge of impatience to let people know you're a player.

First, determine the right time to terminate. This requires you to pay attention to the conversation, and recognize when things are starting to slow down or drifting into areas unrelated to the topic at hand. Are you starting to repeat yourself? Have you meandered into talking about personal illnesses, pets, politics or gossip? Are you starting to repeat yourself? Are you enduring long periods of silence filled only by moments of uncontrollable panic? Are you starting to repeat yourself?

As soon as you realize that your conversation has reached a point of diminishing returns – or that both you and your caller have suddenly lapsed into meaningless psychobabble – it's time to take your bows and exit stage right – *before* they do!

Here are some time-tested exit lines:

"I've got to take another call."

"I've got a conference call scheduled in two minutes."

"I've got to get to a screening."

"I've got to be across town in twenty minutes."

"Someone just came into my office."

"I'm on a deadline right now."

"I'm in the middle of negotiations."

"I'm already late for a meeting."

"My lawyer's calling. I've got to take this."

Or the classic of all not-so-subtle blow-offs:

"I'm gonna let you go now."

You may want to modify these lines to fit your personal situation. Specificity also helps...

"I've got to be at Paramount in ten minutes."

"I've got to fax this scene rewrite to Disney by 5:00."

"A writer just showed up for a meeting."

All of these lines, true or not, carry powerful subliminal messages. They all communicate the fact that you're a busy person: other people require your attention. They also communicate a certain degree of impatience: you can't waste your time yapping on the phone when other, more important matters require your attention. Finally, a line such as "I'm gonna let you go now" also suggests that you're doing the caller a favor. And only powerful people are in a position to grant favors.

Now, in addition to these "blow-offs," you probably want to add some request for, or assurance of, future action. For example, if you're a writer and you've been discussing story notes, you should say something like, "I'll get right on it" or "I'll have new pages over to you by the end of the week." If you're a producer or a director talking to a writer, you might say something like, "Get me those new pages as soon as you can," "Let me know how things are going," or "Call me if you have any problems." If you received the call, rather than instigated it, you might also thank the caller for his/her attentiveness. "Thanks for calling," you might say. Or, "It's always good to hear from you."

So, by combining these lines and variations thereof, you have an almost endless supply of elegant conversation-enders:

"I've got another call I have to take. I'll get right on it."

"I have to be over at Universal in ten minutes. Get me those notes as soon as you can."

"I've got to get to a lunch meeting. But thanks for calling."

"I'm gonna let you go now. But let's meet for lunch real soon."

We could go on like this forever, but our agent's on the phone. We really have to take this. We'll see you in the next chapter.

HOLLYWOOD RULE #13: DON'T DATE ANYONE IN THE INDUSTRY, UNLESS...

Many aspiring writers, producers and directors believe that dating – or even marrying – someone in the motion picture industry is a really nifty idea. By definition, the two of you will have something in common. You'll both have a companion who intimately understands the whipsaw nature of this highly capricious business. Screenings make for a cheap date. And, who knows, it might even further your career.

In a way, this reasoning makes sense. We've discussed at some length how Hollywood is built on a foundation of personal relationships; what could be more personal than sex? And Hollywood has always had its share of successful filmmaking couples, from Cruise-Kidman to scribes Nick Kazan and Robin Swicord to producers Richard and Lili Fini Zanuck and Anne and Arnold Kopelson. The precedent does exist.

But while a few select filmmaking twosomes have managed to keep both their marriages and careers intact, dating someone in the industry – like Acapulco cliff diving or eating an Oldsmobile – is not something we can recommend in good conscience. Basically, it comes down to another old adage, "Don't shit where you eat." Half of all marriages break up, and the attrition rate for "casual" relationships is so high that statisticians don't even bother to keep count. You're going to make enough enemies just by being successful. Do you really need to add a gaggle of angry ex-lovers to the mix, especially when he or she may be in a position to kill your next project before it can even go into development?

(A cautionary tale concerning high-profile showbiz marriages can be found in the story of producers Michael and Julia Phillips. In the 1970s, their collaboration produced the Academy Award-winning Best Picture *The Sting*, and the classics *Taxi Driver* and *Close Encounters of the Third Kind*. But their greatest fame grew out of their subsequent break-up and individual career tailspins, the specifics of which were detailed in Julia's best-selling 1991 tell-all *You'll Never Eat Lunch in This Town Again*.)

Of course, when you're a filmmaker, it's often very difficult *not* to date someone in the movie business. Those of us who've chosen film as a career tend to be driven, obsessive, pathetically myopic individuals who eat film trivia, drink industry gossip, and dream about box-office stats. We *love* this business, warts and all, and will naturally be attracted to kindred spirits. Face it, when your whole life revolves around high concepts, A-list casting and weekend grosses, you're not likely to have a whole lot in common with a computer networking engineer or a hairstylist. Like seeks like.

Also, if you're active in the Business, chances are the only people you'll see on a regular basis are other industry people. Working filmmakers put in *long* hours and rarely have time to develop a full, satisfying social life outside of work. So they tend to make work their social life. This is particularly true for people working in television or on location shoots. These experiences tend to be extremely intense, and intense emotions inevitably lead to men and women turning to each other for comfort, support, and nookie. "On-set romances" between stars are a staple of the gossip columns and supermarket tabloids. Far less publicized are trysts between behind-the-scenes personnel; but they are just as common, if not more so.

All romantic relationships are fraught with potential pitfalls, and the high-stakes nature of filmmaking only amplifies these dangers. For one, when a man and woman meet on a project, it may very well be that the only thing they have in common *is* the project. This is fine for a while, since the project is likely to be all consuming. Once the project has been completed, however, it's common for couples to realize there's nothing else that binds them together. Disentanglement is always a messy business, and the fact that you're dealing with two passionate, strong-willed, and opinionated people – the only kind that work in Hollywood to begin with – only makes matters stickier.

Another way to put yourself in harm's way is to date a studio executive or other authority figure, regardless of how limited their authority might be. When the relationship is hot, there's the danger that any help your significant other might give you could be construed as favoritism due to the fact that you're sharing a bed. Your talent won't be judged on its own merits. And when you break up – as most couples eventually do – your ex might just be vindictive enough to poison your entire relationship with his or her organization. Even a mere "reader" has the power to say "No" to a script before it ever gets to those people who are in a position to say "Yes." Oh, sure, many relationships end amicably, and some ex-lovers even manage to continue working on a professional basis. But why take the chance?

The most daunting challenges that face intra-industry couples are conflicting work schedules and professional envy. It's always difficult for working couples to find time for one another, but the problems increase exponentially when the partners are each working fourteen-hour days, night shoots, and going on location for months at a time. You think being in a relationship with a doctor is difficult? Try dating someone working on the latest *Star Wars* movie. And then there's the classic *"A Star is Born* Syndrome," where the man's career is eclipsed by the woman's, or vice versa. Unless both careers are progressing at the same pace – and this rarely happens – the results are likely to be jealousy, acrimony, and name-calling. (We're sorry if this is all starting to sound familiar.)

Those few intra-industry relationships that *do* work tend to be between people whose jobs are significantly dissimilar. For example, a director and an actor may be able to make a go of it. Or a producer and an editor. Or a writer and – well, we all know how hard it is to live with a writer! The trick is to find someone with whom you're emotionally, intellectually, spiritually, and sexually compatible – yet with whom there's little personal competition, little chance for serious professional retribution should things blow up in your respective faces.

When all is said and done, dating someone entirely outside of the industry may be the best route. After all, "I'm in the movie business" is a great pick-up line; but only *outside* Hollywood, a place where everyone else is *not* in the movie business.

HOLLYWOOD RULE #14: MAKE THE MOST OF HOLLYWOOD PARTIES

The Hollywood Party is a celebrated Los Angeles institution. Immortalized, satirized, and demonized in such classics as Blake Edwards' *The Party* (1968), Woody Allen's *Annie Hall* (1977) and Robert Altman's *The Player* (1992), it is a gathering where movieland insiders and wannabes come to mingle, imbibe, talk shop, dish dirt, and secure temporary bed partners. Although a party is, by definition, an event at which you're supposed to relax, kick back and enjoy yourself, in truth the Hollywood Party is as ritualized as the Pitch Meeting or Doing Lunch. It's a place fraught with danger and possibilities, where careers can be launched or ambitions dashed. At the Hollywood Party, you can sail like *Titanic* or crash like *Speed 2*.

Hence the need for the good old *Hollywood Rules*.

Although Hollywood parties occur in numerous styles, shapes and forms, most can be assigned to either of two major categories: Formal and Informal. The Informal is by far the most common. These tend to be held at someone's home or office and permit you to come and go virtually at your own leisure. You can arrive at any time, as long as you're *fashionably late*, stay from anywhere to a few minutes to several hours, and depart at your convenience, as long as you're *not the last to leave* (unless you're dating the host). Attire at such events tends to range from grubbies to work clothes to borderline formal. Some folks will have come from the office while other people will have come from the beach. Expect to wear and see a lot of black.

During your early years in Hollywood, most of the parties you'll attend will be of the informal variety. Only when you reach a certain level of success will you begin to attend Formal parties. These tend to be charity events, celebrity birthday bashes, celebrations held in conjunction with motion picture premieres, and soirees that coincide with such awards as the Oscars, Emmys and Golden Globes. Such parties usually are held in hotels or formal banquet halls. Guests arrive in limousines. Attire ranges from "casual chic" to black tie for men, and "glitz" to designer gowns for women. The paparazzi are ever present. The parties make the society page.

Regardless of the level of party you attend, such events are no excuse to let your guard down. It's not enough to party hardy – you have to party *smartly*. And that means adhering to a strict set of time-tested *Hollywood Rules*.

Again, your arrival should be "fashionably late." If it's an informal party, a half-hour late is early, while an hour to an hour-and-a-half late is basically on time. You want to give the party enough time to rev up, and for your arrival to make the appropriate impression. Being *more* than an hour-and-a-half late will still be construed as *late*, since by this time the party will have likely assumed its own dynamic and it may prove difficult to slip into the mix. And after two hours, many people will have begun to leave, which means you may lose chances to make important contacts.

Formal parties are stricter. Since they're usually run on a timetable – with a movie scheduled to be shown at a certain time, or awards waiting to be handed out – you have far less leeway as to when you can arrive and depart. Basically, you have about a fifteen-minute window of opportunity to arrive, and you leave when everyone else does. Leaving an informal party early merely suggests you're a busy person with numerous social and/or professional obligations. Leaving a formal party early is just plain rude.

When you're at a party, you don't want to mill about. At best you'll look lost, at worst you'll look like a carrion feeder out hunting for scraps. Instead, choose a spot – preferably one where you're well lit – and hold it. And don't just stand alone. Have at least one person by your side (preferably someone within the industry). Then make people come to *you*.

Search out someone friendly, introduce yourself, and then let him/her introduce you to the other hangers-on as the evening progresses. We are, after all, judged by the company we keep. Don't be shy about approaching stars, famous producers or directors. If these people didn't want to talk, they wouldn't have come to the party. To break the ice, compliment their work. No one tires of praise, no matter how rich and famous. If at all possible, find out who'll be at the party *before* you go. That way, you can have the celebrities' credits at your fingertips, ready to hurl the aforementioned compliments. If you don't see any celebrities about, or if they've been "taken" by people who got to them first, go for the couch. Sooner or later, people will get tired and need to sit down – *next to you*. Have a big plate of food in front of you. When someone sits down, offer to share. If there's no couch, then stand near the food or alcohol. At some point during the evening, you'll meet everyone at the event.

If the party moves to a bedroom, be the first one to sit on the bed (for some reason people are hesitant about being the first to do this). Then chill. It shows you're secure with your environment. Everyone will want to sit down, but they need someone to take the lead.

Kitchens are another great place to hang out – everyone wants to be near the food – but watch out for bad lighting. Kitchen flourescents can make you look like crap. The good news is that at least everyone else in the kitchen will look like crap too.

For variety's sake, you may want to plant yourself near a bathroom. When people are waiting in line to use the restroom, they tend to be nervous, and nervousness often leads to conversation. Also, areas near bathrooms tend to be quieter, more private, and thus more conducive to conversation than crowded living and dining areas.

Now let's discuss a somewhat delicate matter: leaving with a member of the opposite sex. This is, after all, a key reason why many people attend parties, industry or otherwise. If you plan on getting laid that night, don't drive to the party. Go with a friend or, if he/she is on the intoxicated side, take a taxi. When it's time to leave, you can offer to accompany your intended home. Very efficient. And *never* drive drunk – it's too easy to get killed this way. Throughout Hollywood history, we know of many whom have died this way. Also, by being sober, you're in a position to do someone of importance a favor...or get laid.

Being a post-party leader can be very important. When the party is drawing to a close, those people who are still on their feet will no doubt start talking about what to do next. Be the person who comes up with the best suggestion. Don't wait and follow the crowd. Be a leader! Demonstrate your initiative, creativity and showmanship. These are, after all, the qualities everyone looks for in a filmmaker.

Of course, as in any social situation, it's important that you be witty, gracious, charming and civil. You may be surprised at how hard it is for some people to "mind their manners" once they get a few drinks in them. The tabloids and gossip shows are never at a loss for stories about stars who get into drunken brawls, cold-cock pesky photographers, or drive their Porsches into someone's swimming pool. Recently, the Hollywood press (including the business section of the *L.A. Times*) was abuzz about a flashy, well-known studio executive who dropped his drawers smack in the middle of a pre-Academy Awards bash and had a sweet young thing do a Monica Lewinsky on his Little Oscar. Afterwards, the rueful consensus was that the man "needed help." (Although it appears he was already getting all the help he needed.)

The point is, you want to build a reputation in Hollywood, but you want it to be the *right* reputation. People branded as "flakes" or "wackos" can still get work, but it's usually *despite*, not because of, these pejorative monikers. So have fun, but keep your wits about you. In the land of the drunk and stoned, the sober man is king.

HOLLYWOOD RULE #15: KNOW HOW TO WORK A RESTAURANT

If the Hollywood Party is the most celebrated of filmdom's rituals, then Doing Lunch is a very close second. Restaurants are where agents schmooze with clients and buyers, where writers pitch their storylines, where directors impress producers with their grand visions, and where studio execs do whatever it is that studio execs do – all over nourishing food and drink. In a sense, Doing Lunch is the modern equivalent of ancient warring factions declaring peace by "breaking bread" over a common table. Only today, it's multi-million-dollar movie deals being brokered over cheeseburgers, poached salmon, and Chinese chicken salads. And it's all tax-deductible (or better yet...expensed).

Naturally, there are rules about how to Do Lunch. *Hollywood Rules*. They apply if you're dining with professional comrades, potential business partners, studio "suits", or even by your lonesome. The result of countless years of trial-and-error, and tested in eateries from Burbank to Santa Monica, the rules exist for one simple reason: to help you take advantage of every situation that may help you further your career.

The first thing you must consider when Doing Lunch is your choice of restaurant. Of course, you want to choose an eatery where movie people hang out. You want to see important people and *be* seen *by* important people. You want to become a familiar face to even the casual observer. If you and a buddy/potential collaborator are trying to determine where to eat, being able to name several industry hot spots will immediately establish you as a viable player – or, at least, someone with good taste.

What are the current "hot" restaurants? Well, the list of "in" eateries tends to change as frequently as the list of Top 10 movies. But there are several mainstay places you definitely want to frequent. In Beverly

Hills, these include Chasen's (the new one), Barney's, Matsuhisa, Kate Mantilini's (a favorite with ICM), The Grill, Mr. Chow's (a haunt for William Morris agents), The Mandarin, The Peninsula (bar only), Cafe 8 1/2 (also popular with ICM), and Nate & Al's (the city's most celebrated deli). The Midtown area boasts several notable industry hangouts, including Chaya Brasserie (very big with folks at New Line), Indochine, Orsos, The Ivy, Newsroom, Atlantic, Sushi Roka, and The Four Seasons Hotel (bar only). In Hollywood proper, sure bets include Pinot (tops with guys at Paramount), Jones, Formosa Cafe, Ca' Brea, and Musso and Frank's (the last of the classic Hollywood eateries). West Hollywood currently has only one "industry" restaurant, The Palm. Likewise, Culver City can boast of only one true moviemaker Mecca, Bamboo, where the folks at Sony Pictures go to nourish themselves. In Santa Monica, the choices are more varied. There you have Remi, Ocean Avenue Seafood, Icugini, and Ivy at the Shore. Finally, if you're doing business in the Valley, you can take your pick of Cafe Med, El Sole, Hampton's, Art's Deli, Jerry's Deli, Hara Sushi, and Nozowa.

If you're meeting your dining companion at the site, try to show up on time. This way, if your lunching partner is late, it puts you in a position of power. (They will feel they did something to inconvenience you.) But *never be late*. People resent having their time wasted...especially when they're hungry.

If possible, select a table with a good view of the rest of the restaurant, particularly the entrance. If you can see everybody else, it means everybody else can see *you*, which is always desirable. Being able to see the entrance gives you maximum intelligence on who else of importance may be dining there as well.

If you see people you know sitting at another table, acknowledge them with a simple wave. Don't interrupt their meal to say "hi." It's boorish. If someone is waiting alone – and you're alone – it's okay to go over and engage in some quick chitchat. But don't dawdle, and never sit unless invited to do so. If *you're* approached, that's okay. Power attracts. Stand and greet your visitor. If you're dining with guests, be sure to introduce everyone. Make the exchange quick – you never want to ignore the people you're with.

When with someone, don't spend your time fielding calls from your cell phone or looking around the dining area for other big shots. That's plain rudeness. The person you're with already *is* a big shot – why else are you spending time with him? – and deserves all your attention.

Of course, you should never approach someone at a restaurant just because they're reading a script or one of the trades. As noted in *Hollywood Rule #7*, anyone who reads this material in public is probably an *aspiring* filmmaker, and therefore not anyone you really need to know.

Alcohol? You should only drink if your guest suggests it. And then, limit yourself to one glass only. You can't afford to lose control during a lunch meeting, or look like a lush. Remember that you're here to conduct business, not tie one on. However, you should always order *something* to drink, even if it's just bottled water. Drinking the ice water they bring to the table will only establish you as a person with no taste. It doesn't matter that they throw a lemon slice into it: tap water, in L.A., can kill you.

Be careful to only order dishes that can be eaten unobtrusively and with little mess. Pasta is always dangerous, especially pasta with marinara sauce. Getting up all those noodles can be tricky, plus it tends to splatter. Very awkward. But penne pasta, fusilli and ravioli can be eaten with ease. Big fat sandwiches can also be troublesome, unless you're adept at taking small, delicate bites. Nothing will make you look more like a goon than trying to talk with a mouth full of meat, cheese, lettuce and a hunk of thick, crusty bread.

Never go to the bathroom at the end of a meal. This makes it look like you're trying to avoid paying the check. No one likes a cheapskate. In fact, you should always offer to pay for the meal – and immediately demur if your host counter-offers. In point of fact, your host *should* pay. He is probably far wealthier than you at this point in your career. Again, if he/she is not, why are you spending the time? However, if you asked someone to lunch, put forth a sincere effort to pick up the tab. If they asked you to lunch and you get stuck with the bill, pay it cheerfully – then never do business with them again. Like we said, nobody likes a cheapskate. That includes you.

There's a lot to remember here, and many people find the whole Doing Lunch experience rather daunting at first. In fact, they sometimes get so nervous that they lose their appetite. To avoid appearing sickly and peaked at lunch, have something to eat first. Doing Lunch is a lot easier if you don't do it on an empty stomach!

HOLLYWOOD RULE #16: ALWAYS TAKE THE MEETING

Meetings are as essential to life in Hollywood as steel bolts are to Boeing Aircraft. Writers meet with producers. Producers meet with other producers. Directors meet with producers, writers and *re*writers. Some meetings take place at the office, some meetings occur in restaurants. A few meetings even take place in one of the principals' homes. And the irony is, most of these meetings will result in... absolutely nothing.

The first time a new writer, producer or director gets an appointment with a studio executive or other Hollywood Big Shot, it's natural to believe that a deal is imminent. "These are busy people," you may think. "They're not going to take the time to meet with me unless they really want to make my film!"

Ah, ignorance is truly bliss.

The truth is, meeting with new talent for the sole purpose of being able *to match a name with a face* is one of the primary responsibilities of producers and studio executives. In most cases, these people have absolutely no intention of buying your script, offering you an assignment, or putting your project into development. They only want to get acquainted and – because they like your work just enough to take you seriously – to "find out what else you've got."

In fact, these words are a clear tip-off that you are in nothing more than a "Get Acquainted Meeting," or what's better known as a "General Meeting." When you're asked, "What else have you got?" or "What are you working on?" it means they're *not* going to buy what you gave them. They do, however, want to get in line for your *next* project, on the off chance they might like it enough to buy it.

In pitch meetings, producers and executives are invariably polite and, in many cases, downright enthusiastic. This is in no way a sign that they're going to actually make a deal with you. As we just explained, their primary job is to build relationships, not buy projects. When they say, "We love your script" it means "No." When they say, "We think your project is great, but we already have something just like it in development" it means "We're already up to our necks with projects that are going nowhere, so unless you've got Tom Cruise or Julia Roberts attached, don't waste our time."

Attend enough of these meetings, and a sense of ennui – if not downright frustration – is bound to set in. Month after month of being told how wonderful you are with nothing to show for it, and you may vow to never go to another meeting unless a real offer is going to be tendered.

Don't let false expectations get the better of you; they could be career-killers. Instead, welcome every chance you get to make new contacts and open new doors. No matter how useless the appointment may appear, Always Take the Meeting.

"But why waste my time?" you ask. "There are only so many hours in a day." If you're a writer, you may think your time is best spent *writing*, not talking to some slick-ass production V.P. about how much you liked *his* last movie. If you're a producer or director, you may feel that pitching ideas to people who have no intention of buying them is not only a waste of time, but risks the danger of having your ideas *stolen* or, at the very least, "borrowed."

The misconception here is that it's even possible to waste time in a meeting. It never happens. Meetings are the connective tissue of Hollywood. When an oak drops 10,000 acorns – only one of which ever becomes a full-grown tree – that doesn't mean that the other 9,999 were wasted. Seemingly individual, insignificant efforts are, in fact, part of a single process designed to bring about a specific result. As any quantum physicist will tell you, there are no certainties in the universe, only odds. You never know where and when luck is going to strike. You may have a deal that you think is a sure thing, only to have it wither and die. Conversely, you may go into what you're convinced is a bullshit meeting and come out with a quarter-million-dollar deal. You just never know.

Which is why you should cheerfully approach *every* opportunity as the chance of a lifetime. If you'll forgive the cliched sports analogy, you can't hit a home run unless you swing the bat. Just because you'll probably strike out is no excuse not to try. You gotta be *in* it to *win* it! Show business is no place for people looking for guarantees. You want a sure thing? Invest in municipal bonds.

So you'll take the meeting, and you'll make the most of it. Here's how...

HOLLYWOOD RULE #17: TAKE THE BEVERAGE

When you enter any office for a meeting, protocol dictates that the receptionist or assistant offer you a beverage. Accept the offer. We don't care if you just downed a six-pack of Diet Pepsi on the way over and now you need to piss like a racehorse. *Always take the beverage.*

Why? Because accepting the beverage immediately puts the studio/production company in a position of serving *you*. For the briefest of moments, it puts *you* in control. It's a position you'll likely never be in again, so make the most of it.

When accepting the offer, be *very* specific about what you want. If you like Coke, ask for a Coke. If they say, "All we have is Pepsi" say "I really prefer Coke." (In fact, if you really like Coke, ask for a Coca-Cola. This lets them know you're being very brand-specific.)

Likewise, don't let them substitute Sprite for 7-Up, or vice-versa. If you want your drink caffeine-free, ask for it.

Not the same for bottled water, however. If you want Evian and they have Arrowhead, take the Arrowhead. Just don't ask for tap water. They'll think you're suicidal, and suicidal filmmakers are a dime a dozen.

And if you've ordered a soft drink, ask for a glass with ice, too. This makes you look like you know what you want.

The point of all this is to show these people that you have your own mind. You're polite, of course, oozing charm out of every pore. But, even regarding an issue as seemingly trivial as soft drinks, *you're not a person to be fucked with!*

Taking the beverage has another important advantage. Drinks make great props. Like the comedian's cigar, the soft drink is an object you can point with for emphasis, or pause to enjoy after landing a punchline. Most important of all, if you're asked a question you're not ready to answer, you can sip on your drink while your mind races to come up with a response. Very Presidential, no?

So remember: *always* take the beverage.

HOLLYWOOD RULE #18: KNOW WHEN TO SHOW UP & WHEN TO SHUT UP

Timing *is* critical to any comic performance. It's also something you must master if you're to have successful pitch meetings. A true *pitch-meister* controls the clock the way Michael Jordan controls a basketball. As a follower of the *Hollywood Rules*, time is yet another powerful weapon in your arsenal.

When timing a meeting, the first thing you need to control is your arrival. *Always* be on time to your appointments. Not early. Being early makes people think you have nothing better to do than park your carcass on their couch and read week-old issues of *The Hollywood Reporter*. Being early also puts the people you're meeting with on the spot. It puts them under pressure, which will not make them happy. So don't show up early.

Conversely, never show up late. (There's no "fashionably late" where meetings are concerned.) Being late makes you look undependable. Movie and TV people have enough to worry about without having to juggle their schedules around people who can't bother to be somewhere when they're scheduled to be.

When preparing for a meeting, always keep in mind that Los Angeles-area traffic is notoriously unpredictable. If you're driving across town, always give yourself plenty of leeway in case the police have closed down a key road to do battle with Uzi-wielding bank robbers, or if there's a toxic waste spill on the freeway. If nothing goes wrong and you arrive early, you can always hang out in the studio commissary or hole up in your car practicing your pitch.

If, despite your best efforts, it looks like you *are* going to be late, *call ahead.* (One reason why everyone in Hollywood has a cell phone.) Chances are, being ten to twenty minutes late won't be a problem. Everyone understands; we've all been there. In this town, being late is never a mortal sin. Not warning people is.

Once you arrive at a meeting, you will invariably be asked to wait in the reception area until the person you're scheduled to meet with becomes available. Again, you must be a master of the clock. If you've been waiting for thirty-five minutes and you still haven't been called in, politely explain to the receptionist that you have to be elsewhere and ask to reschedule the appointment. Do this even if your next appointment isn't until next Tuesday. Time is valuable: let it be known that yours is not to be wasted.

If this looks like it's going to be a *real* hot meeting, or if the person you're meeting with apologizes profusely and begs your indulgence, you may stretch this waiting limit to forty-five minutes. After that, however, bail. Otherwise, you'll look like a sucker. Plus, leaving after you've made the effort to drive across town and then waited for *nearly an hour* puts the producer/executive/agent in a defensive position. He/she will feel bad. And you can milk the situation with a follow-up phone call letting them know you had to reschedule something else due to their tardiness.

But now, let's assume that everything went smoothly and you're in the executive's office. How much time should you spend, and how should you spend it?

Figure you're going to have about thirty minutes. If the meeting runs forty to forty-five minutes, you're doing well. If it runs an hour, you're doing great. But you should only count on thirty.

Your first ten minutes will probably consist of introductory small talk. Find something to compliment. For example, if the company/studio released a picture any time during the last year, that's a good place to begin. If the picture was a hit, compliment their success. This works even if you've never seen the film. There's nothing to be lost by siding with the majority. However, if you genuinely liked the film, compliment it even if it was a commercial bomb. The company/studio itself must have seen something in it, and your willingness to support the project will demonstrate your impeccable good taste. However, if the picture tanked and you hated it, don't even mention it. No one wants to wallow in failure. Instead, talk about how you're looking forward to seeing their *next* film – if you know what it is.

If the executive has toys in his/her office – and being overgrown children, many of them do – you can talk about them, but *never play with them*. That's lowering yourself to their childlike behavior. But if you notice that a toy is knocked over or otherwise askew, you're free to straighten things up. It's nice to show an exec that you'll take care of him/her like a parent.

Fashion is another excellent subject about which to fire off a compliment, but you've got to know what you're talking about. Always compliment upwards. If it's Armani Express, make sure you thought it was Gucci. If you can nail the designer, call it – unless it's K-Mart or The Gap.

After the initial exchange of compliments, you'll probably be asked "So what are you up to?" Or, if this is an initial introduction, "Tell me about yourself." Keep this response short and sweet. In other words, don't bring up other meetings (even if they ask) or other people you've met with. Keep all your answers relevant. No one is interested in your Aunt Molly's varicose vein operation.

All told, this introductory segment should last about ten minutes. Any longer than that and you're wasting time – the exec's *and* yours. It's time to get down to business! If you're there to discuss a project you've submitted, get to it. If you're there to pitch an idea, pitch away.

When talking about a previously submitted script or project package, the discussion will be free form, with equal amounts of give and take between all the parties present. You'll talk. They'll talk. They'll talk some more. You'll listen. After about twenty to twenty-five minutes, you may feel the energy in the room starting to wane. If so, it's time for you to take control. Tell everyone how well you think the meeting has gone, review the salient points, and then be on your way. Don't let the people you're meeting with be the ones to bring down the curtain. This is a sure sign that you've overstayed your welcome. Better to make them think you've got a lot of other irons in the fire, and they've been lucky to see you for as long as they have. As in *Hollywood Rule #12*, Always leave 'em wanting more.

If you're pitching a project, keep your presentation down to five or ten minutes. At this point, no one wants to know all the details of your story. They want to know the premise, the set-up, the conflict, two or three major plot twists, and then the climax and resolution. They want to know who the hero is, who the villain is, and who the love interest is. Period.

When making a pitch, carefully watch your listener's eyes. If they begin to glaze over or wander around the room, you know you're in trouble. Move ahead quickly. In Hollywood, you can freely insult people, betray them, and swindle them out of their last penny. Just don't bore them.

It's never a good idea to stay seated during an entire pitch. You should stand at least once. This gives your presentation visual variety and physical energy. However, only stand to dramatize appropriate story points. Don't jump to your feet just for the hell of it. This makes you look immature, maybe even a bit scary.

You should be prepared to offer at least two ideas at any pitch meeting. If one fails to generate interest, you should have an immediate backup. After all, you may not get another appointment for another two months. *But*, never come in with more than two ideas. First, your execs probably won't have time to hear more than two. Second, give them more than two ideas and they'll get confused. Three or four stories are too many to handle at one time. Rather than choose just one, they'll choose *none*. Finally, if you come in with a boatload of ideas, it suggests that you've been generating stories no one's been buying. Too many ideas devalues them all. Finally, make sure your pitch is given with passion. We all knew someone growing up who had the ability to make a bathroom visit as exciting as a 007 flick. And passion can sometimes compensate for a weak story.

All too frequently, during your meeting the producer/exec you're talking to will be interrupted by one or more phone calls. If the call is short, this is not a problem. But if the call is long, you're entitled to take it personally. After all, you're busy too! If it looks like the exec is going to be on a while, don't just sit there like an idiot. Ask to use the guest phone (or, if unavailable, your cell phone) and make one or two calls of your own. Call up a friend. Call your answering machine. Just don't call your agent. (This is like calling your mom during sex.)

As soon as the exec gets off the phone, you should too. Then it's back to business. The point is to impress upon the exec that your time is also valuable, although you do respect the time he/she is giving you.

Again, always be the one to terminate the meeting. Thank them for their time, promise to stay in touch, then make a hasty exit. Never hang around the office. And don't ask for a parking validation. Take it if it's offered, but don't inquire; it makes you look cheap. You can, however, ask the receptionist on your way out. (This may end up being the only validation you'll get!)

If you've managed your time well, you should be in and out in forty-five minutes – tops. The people you've met with will be impressed not only with your talent, but also with your efficiency. After all, time is money. Money is power. And – have we mentioned this? – Power is *Everything*.

HOLLYWOOD RULE #19: ALWAYS HAVE A PROJECT IN HAND

Going to meetings and schmoozing with producers and studio people can be lots of fun. You get to sit in nice offices, see lots of old framed movie posters, and enjoy plenty of free drinks. But it's all pointless unless you're prepared to give these people something they *want*. And we're not talking about your talent, regardless of how vast it is. No, we're talking about a *project* these people can run with.

In most cases, this means a finished script that – all things being equal – is ready to shoot. If you're a writer, this is *your* script. If you're a producer or director, it's a script you've optioned *from* a writer. If there's a big-name star or other major element attached, so much the better. But there must be something concrete, something tangible. And it should be so good that, even if they don't particularly like *you*, they'll want to make it anyway. You'll just happen to be one of the costs that comes with it.

Having a "project in hand" when you go into a meeting (and we're not talking about actually having it in hand) may seem like an obvious strategy, but you'd be surprised at how many people forget this basic *Hollywood Rule*. All too often, an executive will be impressed with a screenplay and call its writer, producer or director into a meeting. They'll schmooze for a while, then the executive will say, "We really like this project, but we've got something similar already in development. What else have you got?" At this point, the anxious filmmaker will mistakenly respond with "I'm working on another one right now" or "I'm putting something together" or "We're just finishing up our first draft."

The single translation for all these responses is one simple word: NOTHING. If you don't have another project ready to go, you've got nothing. Zilch. Zip. *Bupkes, baby!*

Imagine: Here you stand before someone in a position to actually move your career forward, and you've got nothing to give him. It's a blown opportunity you may never recover.

How do you avoid finding yourself in this untenable position? If you're a producer or director, you should be developing several projects simultaneously. You should constantly be on the lookout for strong, exciting scripts and stockpile as many as your budget can afford. Steven Spielberg and James L. Brooks didn't get where they are by devoting years to nurturing and developing a single pet project. They've always had their fingers in multiple pies, sometimes juggling many at once. In a town where the odds are always against you, it's the only way to get ahead.

If you're a writer responsible for generating your *own* material, this gets a little harder. The natural temptation is to write a screenplay, then immediately send it to market. Although you can always get lucky and make that million-dollar deal, it's in your best interest *not* to market *that* spec script until you have a second spec script ready to go as well, or close to it.

There are two advantages to this strategy. First, if your first screenplay doesn't sell to a particular studio but they do like the writing, they'll likely call to ask the inevitable "What else have you got?" Of course, you always have the option of pitching a new idea, but unless you're very good at pitching – and most people are not – this will get you nowhere. You could also pull out an older script, if you're a writer, but if it's already been around town, chances are there's still old coverage in someone's hard drive that could sink it regardless of its artistic merits. Sometimes changing the title can be enough to mask the script's history; but if you have a brand *new* script that no one's seen before, the executive is going to sit up and take notice. For not only is this fresh, untainted material, but the executive will believe he's being given that all-important "first look," which will make him feel very important indeed! (You, of course, will do nothing to diminish the impression that he's the first to see this new opus.) Plus, there's an unspoken pressure to purchase the project for a large sum of money, so you're inviting them to make the deal before you take it elsewhere.

There's another reason to always have a second backup script available. If, by some miracle, your first project *does* sell, you will quickly – and temporarily – be in very high demand. This is called becoming a "Flavor of the Month." You'll have a very brief and limited window in which to take advantage of your hot status. (This is as true for producers and directors as it is for writers. If your name makes the trades as being attached to a just-sold project, you're hot. Everyone will want to be in business with you. Success breeds success.)

If you have a second project ready to go, you can get people to read it right away and – because you're now on everyone's minds – your chance of selling it suddenly doubles. The price you can command also rises commensurately.

If you wait two or three months *before* finishing your next script, the heat you are lucky enough to have will cool off considerably, and you may find yourself back at square one. So resist that urge to strike out with the first good thing you've got. Like heads, two projects are better than one.

HOLLYWOOD RULE #20: REJECTION: LEARN TO LOVE IT

So, you've gotten your project into the market, taken plenty of meetings, and what's happened? Well, if you're like 99.9% of the people currently shopping scripts and showing reels around Hollywood, probably not much. There have been no offers, no bidding wars, no million-dollar contracts waved in your face. You've gotten plenty of free beverages and maybe even a lunch or two, but beyond that, you're starting to feel like you've got a Biohazard symbol tattooed on your forehead.

Welcome to Hollywood, Sparky.

Being among the most competitive industries in the world, motion pictures and television are a jamboree of setbacks and disappointment. In his autobiography *The Ragman's Son*, Hollywood legend Kirk Douglas notes that actors had better love rejection, because that's what they're going to get most of their lives. The same can be said for writers, producers and directors. As you might expect, rejection is a constant companion for those people starting out in Hollywood, but it's just as familiar to seasoned pros with a dozen hits under their belts. Rejection is itself one of Hollywood's biggest industries. At this very moment, there are thousands of people gainfully employed all over town whose principal responsibility is simply to say "*No.*"

(Not only will they tell *you* "No," they'll tell their associates and friends they told you "No" to boot. The social and business scenes continually transcend.)

With thousands upon thousands of scripts being shoved at them every year, it's physically and financially impossible for studios to buy, develop and produce even a fraction of the projects they consider. If there are one thousand scripts chasing ten production slots, or if fifty directors are campaigning for the same single assignment, a lot more people are going to hear "No" than "Yes." It's inevitable.

If you want to better calculate the odds against you, consider these numbers. If all things were equal, the 35,000 scripts registered annually with the Writers Guild of America would each have about a 20-to-1 shot of being considered for the 1,500 to 2,000 development slots that get filled by the studios and major independent production companies during any twelve-month period. But, of course, things are never "equal." About ten percent of the films produced each year are either sequels like *Alien: Resurrection*, or *Lethal Weapon 4*, or franchises like the James Bond, Indiana Jones and *Star Trek* series. If you're a newcomer, the closest you'll ever come to one of *these* projects is the ticket you buy at your local octoplex. Another fifteen percent or so of the movies released annually are either remakes of older movies (*Dr. Dolittle, Psycho, The Out-of-Towners*), or classic TV shows (*The Addams Family, The Brady Bunch, Lost in Space*). Many others are ideas that the studios hatch themselves in-house. Again, you've got about as much chance of getting your hooks into one of these projects as David Duke has being named the NAACP's Man of the Year. Of the remaining projects that make it to "A Theater Near You", more than half are written, produced and/or directed by veteran professionals with a long list of previous credits. Studios like to work with people they know. Go figure.

Together, all of these factors combine to increase the odds against you from about 20-to-1 to something closer to 50-to-1. And this is before we even begin to even consider such variables as your proposed movie's budget versus the company's resources, any similar projects the company may already have in the pipeline, the perceived market appetite for your project's particular genre, its marketability both domestically and abroad, and finally, whether or not your project is actually any damn good.

And this is why, no matter *what* you submit, the response you'll probably get is "No."

(Actually, studio executives never say "No." They say, "It's wonderful," "It's great," "I loved it," and "I wouldn't change a word." In a town built on relationships, these are phrases "suits" employ to make sure you come back to them with your *next* project. But unless such praise comes with a solid offer attached, it all has the same meaning: "No.")

But *understanding* "No" and *accepting* "No" are two very different matters. Our mind may tell us that rejection is to be expected, but our gut rebels against it. When we truly believe in a project, we tend to react to a "pass" the same way we would if our doctor told us we had only a month to live. We take it very, very personally.

Taking our cue from the classic Five Stages of Death, here are the *Hollywood Rules'* Five Stages of Rejection:

DENIAL   *"I don't believe you passed on this project.*
It's a brilliant piece of work! It's got
'franchise' written all over it! There must
be some mistake!"

ANGER   *"You moron! You Idiot! I bet you passed on*
Men in Black *too, didn't you? Hell, you*
wouldn't know a hit if it bit you in the ass!"

BARGAINING   *"Okay, so if I cut ten pages, add a new*
subplot, and change the setting from modern
day New York to 16th Century Japan, would you
buy it then?"

DEPRESSION   *"This project sucks. Why'd I even bother?*
The premise is absurd; the structure's got more
holes than Sonny Corleone's corpse, and
Paramount just bought the exact same
story for $500,000 against $1.5 million. I'm
doomed."

ACCEPTANCE   *"All right, so it didn't sell. I've still got*
my health! What's next?"

The trick, of course, is passing through these stages as quickly as possible.

Some people never get past Denial. They keep plugging away on the same project, taking it back again and again, month after month, year after year, in the mistaken belief that the script is letter perfect and that it's the producers and/or studio executives who are the problem. They figure that, with studio turnover the way it is, sooner or later a champion will appear who will be sympathetic to their cause. It rarely happens.

Or they'll go completely the other way and conduct endless rewrites on the project. Better to leave a dead horse alone.

Other people get stuck in the Anger phase. They spend their days railing against the incompetence, crassness, and insensitivity of the marketplace – which in the end makes about as much sense as criticizing the sky for being blue. The market is what it is.

Bargaining is the trap of the truly desperate. They badger their would-be buyers to reveal some magic "fix-it" that will instantly make their project salable, never realizing that if the target company had any *real* interest, they'd at least option the script for a rewrite. Bargaining in this manner only makes one look foolish – and no one wants to go into business with a fool.

For those people who languish in Depression, the result is usually artistic paralysis, unbearable self-loathing, and lots of heavy drinking. Many folks who stop here end up leaving the business altogether – if they haven't already wrapped their car around a lamppost or O.D.'d on the latest *drug du jour.*

No, only by reaching Acceptance are you able to pick up the pieces and move on. Only through Acceptance can you finally achieve the success you seek.

"But what does this 'Acceptance' entail?" we hear you ask. *"Does it mean I toss out a project as soon as it's rejected, only to move on to one project after another like some literary Lothario?"*

Of course not. Our works are our children, and we don't abandon them without a fight. The trick to handling rejection is learning how to make it *work for you.* Here are some tips:

Realize that failure is not an event, but a part of the process. At the same time Babe Ruth led major league baseball in home runs, he was also one of the sport's strikeout kings. Thomas Edison failed hundreds of times before he finally perfected the electric light bulb.

In the same way, a filmmaker must explore multiple dead ends before finding the proper "home" for any particular project. No single submission is the be-all-and-end-all of a script or pitch, nor does any single script or pitch represent the fate of an entire career.

We recently heard a story about a real estate agent who was bemoaning the fact that a house she'd had on the market for six months still hadn't sold. She considered herself a failure. Her manager asked her how many people have to inquire about an average house before it sells. "About fifty," she replied. "Fine," her manager said. "The cost of any 'Yes' is fifty 'No's.' Until you acquire those fifty 'No's, you're not going to be able to sell that house. So you'd better start earning those rejections."

In the same way, the cost of getting a "Yes" on a screen project – even a *good* screen project – is usually around fifty "No's. So seek out those rejections. Look at them as money in the bank. The more you accumulate, the closer you are to getting your "Yes!"

Look for patterns in the rejections you receive. It's damned hard to pry honesty from people in Hollywood – particularly people you know only on a professional basis. But if you can manage to get some truthful critiques of your proposals, you can use them to modify your current project or make future ones more marketable.

However, you must be very careful here. No single comment is ever gospel; you need to look for patterns. For example, let's say you submit a screenplay to four different people. Critic #1 likes the characters, but thinks the plot is thin. Critic #2 says the main plot is okay, but she doesn't like one of the subplots. Critic #3 objects to the story's political overtones. And Critic #4 thinks the script is perfect the way it is. What do these reactions tell you? Absolutely nothing. Try to revise your project to satisfy all your readers and the only thing you'll have is a formless mess. At this point, you're better off just plowing ahead and trusting your own instincts.

But what if three of the four critics agree that the script's ending is weak, and that the entire third act needs to be reconstructed? Now you've got something. Even if you've always thought that the third act was a masterpiece, you'd better take another look and maybe even make some changes. When most people say the same thing – like chocolate mint chip is a great ice cream flavor, and watermelon is not – they're probably right. As someone looking to grab the largest possible audience, you're a fool to ignore the opinion of the majority.

Make your anger productive. Rejection can be a devastating thing. It can also be a great motivator. The people who tend to fail in this business, and there are many, are those who either take rejection so personally that they become gun-shy, or who become so cynical that they simply stop trying. The successful ones are those who respond to a rejection with a defiant "Oh, *yeah?*" attitude, then immediately throw themselves right back into the fray, determined to prove their critics wrong. They not only sneer at rejection; they turn right around and punch it in the kisser.

It takes a tremendous amount of self-confidence – not to mention pure ego – to be able to react with such bravado after repeated pummelings, but then Hollywood has never been known for its modesty and self-effacement. You must learn to take each rejection as a challenge, to view every setback as a gauntlet thrown at your feet. Take that rage and channel it into your *next* attempt. It may very well give you the edge that finally pushes you over the top.

Never forget: it only takes one. There may be hundreds of listings in the *Hollywood Creative Directory*, but it only takes one buyer to make you a success. A dozen big-time producers and studio execs can say that your project is a piece of crap, but if just *one* says it's great and makes you an offer, suddenly you're golden. A single endorsement immediately negates all objections.

With new production companies being formed every week, with new stars always coming on the scene with the power to give your project cachet, there's never a time when all your options are exhausted. New needles are being tossed into that proverbial haystack every day. All you've got to do is look for them.

Even using these techniques, there may come a dark moment when the situation looks positively hopeless. You may think that you'll never get work in Hollywood, that you'll never see your name on a title card, that all your efforts will turn out to be a pitiful waste.

If you give up at this dark moment, all your efforts really *will* be a waste. It's not like you can take the experiences gained in Hollywood and apply them to other, more "legitimate" endeavors. Putting "Unemployed feature film director," "Producer with no track record," or "Unproduced screenwriter" on your resume won't earn you brownie points at Microsoft or McDonnell-Douglas or McDonald's, for that matter! (Even advertising, public relations, and industrial filmmaking offer you few opportunities. Usually, people use the skills gained in these fields to get *into* the movies, not vice versa.) In the end, about the only place you can exploit what you've learned about Hollywood is *in* Hollywood. So unless you want to write off the last few years of your life, you've really got no choice but to stick with it.

And why not keep trying? In the end, the only person who can ever truly say you've failed is *you*. All paranoid fantasies aside, there's no cabal of industry insiders who are in a position to block your success, even if they wanted to. There's no timetable you must beat or monetary criteria you must meet to be declared either a "winner" or a "loser." And there's certainly no "blacklist" of untouchable writers, producers, and directors whose talent is considered so meager that companies are forbidden to buy their services. In fact – unless you've committed a capital crime – tomorrow you could traipse into a studio bearing the next *There's Something About Mary*, and go from being a nobody to everyone's best friend literally overnight. (Even embezzlement, wifebeating, assault, and persistent drug use have done little to slow the careers of entertainers who are still considered to have "something to offer.")

So, like the Timex watches of old, a student of the *Hollywood Rules* will take each licking and keep on ticking. If you've got any talent at all – and you *know* you do – luck must eventually turn your way.

And what do you do when it does? How do you make the most of success when it finally arrives?

We're glad you asked...

HOLLYWOOD RULE #21: ASK FOR EVERYTHING

Congratulations! All your months – or is it years? – of hard work have finally paid off. At long last, you've found someone who wants to make your movie. *Now* things get interesting.

Based on what you've read in the trades, you may think that at this point someone's going to hand you a check for some ungodly amount of money and sign you for a three-picture deal. You may imagine yourself spending your afternoons lunching with studio bigwigs and your evenings rubbing elbows with movie stars at lavish Hollywood soirees.

You'll likely picture yourself at the wheel of a Lexus or some other auto du jour, and perhaps fantasize about throwing a housewarming party at your new aerie in the Hollywood Hills. At the very least, you figure you'll finally pay off your credit card debts.

Hey, why not? It *could* happen.

But if you're like most industry neophytes, things won't go quite so smoothly. There are apt to be numerous detours and switchbacks on your way to Easy Street. When you get your first offer, your best course of action is to step back, take a deep breath, open your eyes, and prepare to take things very slowly. Your goal now is to make the best of what could be a confusing and even perilous situation. If you play your cards right, you could end up with some very attractive perks. If you're too demure or, conversely, too cocky, you could end up royally screwed. If this makes it sound like you're walking a tightrope, you are. And there's no net.

First, let's understand who you're dealing with, and how your project got where it is.

If your project has gone the way most do, the screenplay in question and a list of attached elements – if any – went to any number of producers around town. It did *not* go directly to the studios. Why not? Because that's the way the system works. Studios prefer their projects to be presented by producers with whom they already have established relationships; they consider those producers' enthusiasm to be a credible endorsement of the project's value. If a Jerry Bruckheimer or a Mace Neufeld wants to make a certain movie, there must be something to it, right? Having a big-name producer attached not only makes the project more attractive to the suits, it also increases its chances of going straight to a top executive empowered to actually make an offer. Without a producer, the script will likely be handed off to a low-paid reader whose job is, in essence, to say "No" and affix the screenplay with a bad report ("coverage") that will haunt it 'til the sun goes nova, the oceans boil away, and our planet withers to nothing but an iceball floating forever through the infinite wastes of cold, empty space. See?

Going to an established producer is usually *de rigueur* even if you're a producer yourself. Most first-time producers lack the clout necessary to deal directly with a Universal, a Paramount, or a Twentieth Century Fox. They need to partner with a Joel Silver or an Arnold Kopelson who can open all the necessary doors and provide the credibility needed to gain a studio's support. This person may or may not be actively involved once production actually commences, but you can bet he'll take a major cut of the proceeds and budget. And your fee and role on the project is negligible next to someone of this stature.

(The need for a "team quarterback" is why you often see such credits as Executive Producer, Co-Producer and Associate Producer attached to feature films. Very often, the Executive Producer is just the Big Shot who puts his name on the project to give it cachet. The Co-Producer or Associate Producer may, in fact, be the person who found the original script and instigated the actual development process – but no more.)

The producer *you* work with will probably operate on one of several levels. He may have an exclusive relationship with a particular studio, which obligates him to make movies for that studio and that studio alone. The upside to this arrangement is that the studio likely puts great stock in what this producer has to say, and if he really wants to make your movie there's a better-than-average chance it will happen. The downside is that if the studio turns it down, there's really nowhere else you can go with it.

Another kind of producer is the one with a "first-look" or "housekeeping" deal at a particular studio. In this case, the studio usually furnishes the producer and his company with offices, either on or off the lot, and a small development fund. In turn, the producer gives the studio the right of first refusal on any new projects he develops. Producers with such deals usually have somewhat less clout than those with exclusive deals. But the advantage is that should their studio pass, they're free to take it to any other studio in town.

A third type of producer is the kind with his own independently financed production company. The money for such companies often obtained through limited partnerships, public stock, or other private financial arrangements (ranging from a rich parent to a retired arms dealer). While most of these producers usually don't underwrite the *total* cost of their own films, they usually have "discretionary funds" large enough to pay for options, rewrites, and even outright screenplay purchases. Actual production costs may or may not be shared with a studio partner. Working with such an autonomous producer often results in a higher level of artistic control since – for much of the development process – the producer alone is the final authority, not some faceless studio committee. However, such a producer's financial resources are often less commanding than those of a major studio, so you may end up paying for your increased artistic control with a smaller paycheck.

Development entities – companies set up to find screenplays for the production entities – are typically created and run by people on the fringe of the industry. These companies are either close to getting a studio deal or simply don't want one. Hopefully they have some discretionary funds to spend on you. And since you're not any more involved in the biz than they are, this arrangement could work for you – especially if they have money to help feed you. Once the project is sold, you'll receive a larger fee.

The final type of producer is the one who has a few credits to his/her name, but who doesn't have his/her own production company, and who has yet to affiliate him/herself with any particular studio. Working with such a "gypsy" producer usually represents the greatest degree of risk, since he's probably operating on little more than his reputation. However, such producers may be more amenable to considering projects from first-time writers, producers and directors, since less of their attention is diverted elsewhere.

So which kind of producer should you work with? Well, the first consideration is simple: Which one's making the offer? The guy who actually wants to produce your movie is immediately more attractive than one who doesn't. Although this may seem obvious, you'd be surprised at how many people set their sights on a certain producer and insist only on working with him/her. "I have to sell this to Spielberg," they might say. Or, "This is a big action picture. It's got to be Joel Silver – or Jerry Bruckheimer." Such naivete is the equivalent of refusing to marry anyone but a Victoria's Secret model or an NFL quarterback.

Standards are fine, but in the end, you have to take what you can get. But let us suppose that two or more producers are vying for your project. Now you have to pick and choose between them. Basically, this comes down to weighing money – both immediate and future – against artistic and personal considerations.

If you truly care about your work, if you're more than just a hack-for-hire, it's important to partner yourself with a producer – or director – you like personally, and who appears to share your artistic vision. If you're going to stay with the project for any length of time, you'll be spending time with this person, so you'd better get along. It also helps to be working toward similar goals.

So now let's say you've found *two* producers or directors who like your project, with whom you feel you can get along, and who appear to share your vision. How do you choose? At this point, again it comes down to money and perks. Who will pay the most? How will these payments be scheduled? And what other benefits or assurances will they offer?

When negotiating contract points, the best strategy is to *ask for everything*. Don't *demand* everything. *Ask*. The worst thing they can do is say "No" (or laugh). In a surprising number of cases, they'll say "Yes" to things you would have never received unless you had raised the issue. Of course, at this point, you should have an agent or lawyer. But they too will attempt to talk you out of asking for some of these points. Encourage them to at least try. What have you got to lose?

What kinds of things should you ask for? For *producers* dealing with other producers, directors, or studios, here's a working list of items you can consider:

Ask for final cut. You ultimately want the picture to conform to *your* vision and no one else's.

Ask for casting approval. The director may voice his choices, but you certainly want veto power. The studio typically gives a list of actors who can greenlight the movie. Review the list together and see if you can agree.

Ask for approval on all major technical personnel: the director of photography, the production designer, the costume designer, the music composer, and the special-effects supervisor, if any. Again, you're not demanding or dictating, just asking for the chance to keep your hand in as much as possible.

Ask for a minimum of 20% of your producer's fee up front. Many producers receive only a pittance until a movie actually goes into production – which can be years after its screenplay is first put into development. Hope is a wonderful thing, but it doesn't pay the rent.

Ask for your own trailer. Stars and directors get them, so why shouldn't you if you're overseeing the production? You're going to be spending a lot of time on the set, and you need a place you can call your own. If you're not involved in the shooting of the movie, and don't have to go to the set to make money, don't. If they don't want you there or don't feel you have a purpose, move on to a new project.

Ask for a percentage of any merchandising based on the movie. This includes not only characters but also symbols, images, vehicles, music, etc. How much do you think Warner Bros. made in 1989 from the Batman symbol alone? Marketing is big business.

Ask for a clause that obligates the studio to pay you more money – plus interest – if they're late with any of their scheduled payments. This should keep 'em honest.

Ask for a clause that requires you to approve all poster designs, TV ads, trailers, and other marketing materials. A great marketing campaign can make a mediocre film a commercial hit (say, *Flubber*), while a poor one can send a worthy product sinking to the bottom (say, *The Shawshank Redemption*). This is an area in which you certainly want to exercise some control.

Ask for the first right to negotiate for the sequel. You made the picture the success it is, so they should *want* you back to rework your magic.

If you're a director dealing with a producer or a studio, the list is similar. Only this time, screw the producer(s). The movie is now *your* baby – *you* are the auteur – and you want to exercise as much power as possible.

Since the '60s, Hollywood has traditionally been *very* accommodating to directors, granting them the supreme position of authority in most matters. But not in *all* matters. So here are the points you want added to your contract:

Ask for the right of final cut. You don't want some meddlesome producer or, even worse, a bunch of studio hacks butchering your work. No one else is going to know your movie better than you do, so you should be the one to dictate its final form.

Ask for a percentage of the gross. Not net profits – which, invariably, never materialize – but a piece of each ticket sold at the box office. Usually, "gross points" are reserved for major directors and big-name stars, but if you're hot enough, you may be able to pull it off.

Ask for a percentage of the merchandising. If this movie succeeds, a lot of the credit will fall to you, so you deserve a piece of any ancillary spin-offs.

Ask for a possessory credit, as in "A John Smith Film" or "A Film by John Smith." Writers and producers *hate* this, but who listens to them anymore? Success in Hollywood depends on *recognition*, and you should go for it wherever you can. However, if you want to build or maintain a relationship with the writer and producer, you may want to share this credit with him/her.

Ask that your name be announced *verbally* in all trailers and radio and television advertising. "Directed by (Your Name Here)" will do much to raise your stock, even if this is just your first feature film.

Ask for the first right to negotiate for the sequel. If the picture's a hit, it's because you *made* it a hit. They owe you.

And what about *writers*? Writers have traditionally gotten the short end of the stick when it comes to dealing with producers, directors, and studios. Where producers tend to stay with a project from beginning to end, and directors are replaced only under the most dire circumstances, a writer's interest in a film can disappear before the ink is even dry on his contract. *Take the Money and Run* isn't just the title of an old Woody Allen comedy – it's the way most writers have learned to do business.

But more and more, writers are fighting to take an increasingly active role in helping to translate their written words into moving images. Here's a list – a *long* list – of things writers can ask for during their negotiations with producers, directors and studios:

Ask for a clause that states you can't be rewritten. You must do any rewriting, and any proposed dialogue changes that occur on the set must be approved by you before they can be filmed. This is the same power that has been enjoyed by stage writers for decades, so it's not without precedent. If you want this control, you must be present for all notes and shooting, and flexible for production restrictions. If you choose to leave a project of your own volition, you give up this control.

Ask for a clause that states that, should you be fired, you will be paid a huge bonus. This will be a disincentive for a producer or director to replace you with one of their cronies.

Ask for director approval and the right to produce at least one additional rewrite (if you don't get script approval) – if necessary – once the director is brought on board. Directors are notorious for bringing in their own writers even after a script is considered "locked down."

Ask that all rights to your original screenplay revert back to you if the movie is not produced during a specified period of time. An alternative to this is to ask for the right to *repurchase* the script for its original option value. Any monies paid to you for rewrites remain yours, as these changes were made at the producer's/studio's request.

Ask that there be no "possessory credit" attached to your movie, unless you are yourself the director. After all, the story originated with you, and the final product is as much yours as it is anyone else's. And if you're not directing, ask for "Meaningful Consultation" on all matters involving the director.

Ask to be guaranteed permission to spend as much time on the set as you would like. If the film is being shot on location, ask for two first-class, round-trip airline tickets to the destination – plus first-class accommodations for as long as you wish to stay there. Also ask that tickets, transportation, and accommodations be provided to all sneak previews, premieres, and festivals where your film will be shown.

Ask for a clause that guarantees that you will be included in all press materials, and that you will be allowed to participate in all press junkets and other publicity activities related to your film. As a rule, writers have been "invisible" during publicity tours, a practice many writers are currently fighting to reverse.

Retain your separation rights, enabling you to protect your future profits in other media, such as TV spin-offs, CD-ROMs, etc. Also, ask for a clause that retains the first right of refusal to pen any and all sequels.

<u>Ask for a percentage of all merchandising income.</u> You created these characters. You deserve a piece of the action.

<u>Ask for gross points in the film and video sales.</u> If you're picture's a hit, even half a point can be worth millions.

Of course, *you're* not the one who will be asking for these things. Your representative will. So don't worry about looking greedy or overly ambitious. That's the job of your agent, manager or entertainment lawyer. And producers expect such avaricious behavior from artists' representatives.

Also, keep in mind that *none* of these items should be considered dealbreakers. They represent best-case scenarios that, in many instances, will be dismissed out-of-hand. (For example, it's extremely rare for writers to get gross points on a film, regardless of their stature within the industry. For a first-time writer, it's unheard of. However, if there are two or more producers or companies vying for your script, your chances of getting this point increase.) By bringing these issues up, you create bargaining chips that you can then surrender in exchange for things you *really* want, or feel you truly deserve. Expecting to get everything your first, second, or even third time out can lead to severe disappointment.

We knew one talented director who, after directing a handful of well-received music videos, was offered a chance to direct a modestly budgeted action film for a major studio. His ego immediately kicked into overdrive and he demanded everything from the right of final cut to his own caterer, personal trainer and masseuse. The studio made an attractive counteroffer, but the director stood firm: he expected to be treated like a king. Realizing they were working with a complete asshole, the studio walked away and found someone else. Despite his acknowledged talent, the director still hasn't broken into feature films. His reputation as an egomaniac will undoubtedly dog him for years.

Now, keep in mind that you'll "ask for everything" *only* if you're in a bidding war situation. When a producer or director steps forward and says he wants to take your project to a studio, he may very well ask for what amounts to a free option. This means that he wants you to give him the exclusive rights to represent your project to one or more specific buyers, in exchange for the time and effort he's willing to put into it. Only when the studio says "Yes" will you be in a position to expect remuneration.

Many people, writers in particular, balk at granting free options. They don't like the idea of putting their futures into someone else's hands, especially since there's every chance that the producer will fail and the project will be permanently "burned" wherever he's taken it. When this happens, all of the writer's work will have been for naught. With a paid option – even if it's just a few thousand dollars – at least one can get back some expenses.

But while paid options are well and good, most producers and directors just don't give them anymore. The spec market is so competitive that there's no pressure to pay advance money to writers. If you're a writer, you must weigh the advantages of partnering yourself with a producer (or director) who carries some clout but will offer no money up front – against holding out 'til someone *does* give you money, which may never occur. Conversely, if you're a producer or director, you can offer to take on a writer's screenplay without having to worry about complex deal memos or shelling out major shekels. With up-front money no longer an issue, all you have to worry about risking is your reputation.

The rules about free options also apply to rewrites. Very often, a producer or director will agree to take on a project *if* certain changes are made to the existing screenplay. The Writers Guild specifically discourages its members from working for free. And they should. When writers don't get paid for their work, the Guild can't collect any dues. However, if you're a writer, working for free may be the only way to get your foot in the door during the early phase of your career. And oftentimes your script will improve by the creative collaboration.

We'll close this chapter with the true story of a talented young writer who came to town bearing a clever but flawed romantic comedy. An established producer with a first-look deal at a major studio liked the project, and offered to help the writer rework the script until it was ready to take to the studio. Eager to make a deal, the writer agreed to a free option and as many free rewrites as were necessary. The two spent eight months reworking the material, during which time the writer received absolutely nothing. Finally, the producer submitted the screenplay to the studio. It sold for $380,000 against $500,000.

Was it worth eight months for free to make $380,000? Granted, it was a risk. And many risks don't pay off. But in Hollywood, you could die of old age waiting for a sure thing. Take the risk.

HOLLYWOOD RULE #22: GET IT IN WRITING

Despite the millions upon millions of dollars that are tossed around this town like so much New Year's Eve confetti, Hollywood can often be a very informal place. Because so many deals grow out of personal relationships, it's not uncommon for producers, directors, and writers to get into projects based on nothing more than a verbal agreement and a firm handshake. Many an $80 million movie has had its origins in drinks shared around a producer's swimming pool, in a poker game held in a director's dining room, or on a writer's driveway basketball court.

But while informality may be a great way to spur creativity, it's a lousy way to do business. And the operative word in show business *is* business, so one should be loath to get too far into what could be a major money venture without formalizing the arrangements.

As soon as you and another party agree to work together – whether it's a producer with a writer, a director with a producer, two collaborating writers, or any combination thereof – the first words out of your mouth should be, "I'll have my agent call your agent and work out the particulars." At which point you should call your agent (or manager or entertainment lawyer), tell him/her the nature of your arrangement *as you understand it*, and indicate the type of written document you'd like produced. It's then up to your representative to work out the specifics with the people representing your collaborator and produce the final document for your mutual signatures.

Early in a project, the agreement need not be a legal tome running dozens and dozens of pages. If it's a contract between two writers, it can be as simple as a deal memo specifying that you agree to split all income produced as a result of your joint efforts on a strict 50-50 basis. If it's the kind of "free option" as discussed in *Hollywood Rule #21*, then the parties might agree that the producer has the exclusive right to represent said script for X number of days to one or more specified studios. A producer might also create a memo in which he agrees that the sales price of a script will be, say, two percent of the film's eventual budget if and when a deal is struck with a studio – half of which will be paid up front upon the signing of formal contracts.

Keep in mind that financial specifics contained in early deal memos often go out the window when a major director, star, or studio steps into the picture. Obviously, the value of a script designed to be produced for, say, $20 million increases substantially if a star like Tom Cruise or Julia Roberts signs on. The film's budget suddenly inflates fourfold. Still, a preliminary deal is useful to keep everyone happy and on the right track during the early stages of a project's development.

"But I'm working with a friend of mine," you might protest. *"Won't asking for a signed deal memo alienate my buddy? Once we start talking about money and who gets what, we're bound to get into arguments. It could ruin our friendship."*

Actually, starting a business relationship with a written agreement is probably the best way to *preserve* a friendship, not undermine one. All too often, two people get along just fine and dandy until wads of money are waved in their faces. Then, like the prospectors in *Treasure of the Sierra Madre*, everyone becomes greedy, paranoid, and resentful. The next step is to argue, throw charges and countercharges, and finally break up. The end result is a movie that never gets made.

When multiple producers are involved – as often happens with spec scripts – getting each one's working parameters in writing can help avoid nasty embarrassments. Recently, a spec attracted so much attention that five different producers wanted to take it to the studios. Since each producer had a different first-look deal, establishing who would do what seemed fairly easy. The producer with a deal at Universal would take it to Universal, etc. In fact, it looked so simple that the agent representing the writer handled the whole thing by phone, with no written documentation. Bad move. One of the producers – let's call him Murray – got an immediate pass from his studio. But he then snuck the script to executives at several other major studios, including the ones already spoken for. Well, you can guess what happened. One of the studios – let's call it Gigantor Pictures – snapped up Murray's project. The problem was, the producer who had the first-look deal at Gigantor thought *he* had exclusive rights to that venue. There was a lot of anger and name-calling; expletives hurled like hand grenades. Lawsuits were threatened. In the end, Murray got his deal and the writer sold his screenplay, but the agent's reputation was damaged, and the scorned producer – who was a respected name in Industry circles – will likely never do business with that agent or that writer again.

Pissing off important people is not a recommended way to launch a Hollywood career.

Both you and your picture have a much better chance of making it through the sales and development process if you establish the ground rules for everyone involved as soon as possible. Getting it all in writing helps avoid any future "misunderstandings" or "misinterpretations," so everyone knows what his responsibilities are and what his eventual rewards are going to be.

If your "friendship" with another person is going to crumble under the strains of your working relationship, it's best to know early, before hours of work have been invested, money has been spent, and other people have been brought into the process. Just as the good ship *Titanic* might have sailed into port had only the lookout been given a pair of five-dollar binoculars, many a creative partnership can be spared the heartbreak of divorce with just one simple piece of paper.

HOLLYWOOD RULE #23: CREATE A PAPER TRAIL

Who are the busiest people in Hollywood? They aren't the writers, the producers, the directors, or even the agents. They're the lawyers. Movies cost money, *lots* of money, and when so much cash is being bandied about, it's only natural for members of the legal profession to be called in to make sure each participant gets his or her proper piece of the pie. (Or to *keep* people from getting their piece.)

As a filmmaker, you stand to make enough dough to choke the proverbial horse. A-list writers can make $200,000 a week just for "punching up" someone else's anemic screenplay. A top director can command two to seven million dollars for his services. A producer can pocket enough change to buy a house just for bringing a hot script to a studio's attention. But at the same time, you can *lose* a king's ransom in this business if you don't protect yourself. And the strongest, cheapest protection is always a piece of paper. Nothing beats a collection of clearly, written records of all your communications, directives and agreements when disagreements turn to litigation.

If you're a writer, proper record keeping begins as soon as you type FADE OUT on the final page of your spec screenplay. The instant your first draft is complete, make two photocopies. Mail one to the Copyright Office of the Library of Congress (contact the Library for the proper forms and current charges), and one to the Registration Office of the Writers Guild of America-west at 7000 W. Third St., Los Angeles, California, 90048. When the Copyright and WGA registration forms are returned, keep them on file. These documents will establish your legal claim to your material, as well as record the date you completed your first draft. If your subsequent drafts contain significant changes, you should register those with the WGA as well. A few bucks spent early on can save you hundreds of thousands of dollars later if plagiarism issues are ever raised.

Regardless of your filmmaking specialty, you should keep written records of all your pitch meetings, including who you met with, the time and date of your meeting, and a brief description of the matters discussed. If you follow up your initial meetings with a written note, keep a copy of that too.

If you agree to a free option to a producer during the sales phase of your project, *get it in writing* and keep a copy on file. Obviously, any other agreements – especially those involving money, no matter how minimal – should be documented.

Once you actually close a deal and contracts are signed, you and your collaborators – including any writers, producers, directors, studio executives, etc. with whom you may be working – will be trading all kinds of correspondence. Dominant among the paperwork will be story notes. It's critical that you not discard these missives once they've served their purpose. Again, keep them on file and well organized.

You need to keep and date all screenplay drafts produced during the development process. This is true even if it takes three years and eighteen separate drafts to get your movie into shootable form. You need to document every step.

Studio notes that arrive during production and post-production also need to be properly filed. These include memos concerning casting decisions, the quality of rushes, scheduling and budgetary concerns, editing suggestions, music notes, marketing strategies, and any other topic relevant to your filmmaking activities.

Looking at this list, you might think that you'll end your film work virtually buried in paper. You will. Which is why you're going to need a *big* filing cabinet.

Why do you have to maintain records with the precision of a Swiss bookkeeper? Because as soon as you start making money in Hollywood, various nasty people will try to take it away from you. (The ones who haven't already tried to keep you from getting it in the first place.)

Here are just some of the problems you can encounter during your Hollywood career that a good set of records can help you resolve in your favor:

Plagiarism. Although it's not a huge problem in Hollywood, every once in a while a writer, producer, director or studio will steal an idea and claim it as their own. If you feel you've been ripped off, being able to document the fact that you submitted your story to the accused – and that he, in fact, read it – can go a long way in proving your case. Conversely, if someone accuses *you* of stealing *his* idea, records of when you wrote and registered your screenplay may be just what you need to establish your innocence and clear your name.

Breach of contract. Substantial payments may be denied to you on the basis that you did not perform your duties as specified in your contract. Your primary defense may lie in written records proving that you did, in fact, fulfill the terms of your agreement. Additionally, you may contend that someone in your employ has failed to do his job, and your position will be significantly strengthened if you can produce a collection of correspondence that proves your ongoing dissatisfaction.

You may recall that, in the early 1990s, humorist Art Buchwald successfully sued Paramount Pictures over monies he claimed he was owed from the creation of the 1988 Eddie Murphy vehicle *Coming to America*. He did not pursue this as a plagiarism suit, but as a breach of contract litigation. During the trial, Buchwald was able to produce a whole stream of memos from various Paramount executives in which his early comedy treatment was discussed and analyzed. Although the resulting movie turned out to be significantly different from Buchwald's original story, it was clear that his treatment was the project's genesis, and that he was owed over a million dollars as a result – in addition to story credit on all future prints of the film.

Around that same time, the producers of the ultimately dreadful suspensor *Boxing Helena* successfully sued actress Kim Basinger over her refusal to star in their movie after having made an oral agreement to do so. Actress Whoopi Goldberg was forced to live up to her agreement to star in the (again dreadful) sci-fi comedy *Theodore Rex* after that film's producers produced evidence that she had verbally committed herself to the project.

Imagine trying to win any of these high-profiled cases without convincing *written* documentation.

Writers Guild Arbitration. If more than one writer is involved in a movie, final credits are determined by a special committee of the WGA. It's up to each writer to submit a copy of every screenplay draft he or she produced. If the arbitrators conclude that a writer contributed at least thirty percent to the eventual screen story (not including dialogue), he or she will be listed as either the sole writer or one of the co-writers. Since a good deal of monetary compensation is dependent upon final credits – not to mention bragging rights – a writer who doesn't keep a copy of everything he's written could very well be cutting his own financial throat.

Of course, it could be that all your filmmaking experiences will go smoothly and you'll never be hauled into court – or have to haul someone else in. If so, God bless you. But, as the saying goes, "better safe than sorry." Keeping detailed records of all your activities and correspondence may be just the thing that saves the career you've struggled so hard to build.

HOLLYWOOD RULE #24: BE EASY TO WORK WITH

Now that you've become a working filmmaker, your primary task is to *remain* a working filmmaker. Like in any business there's getting to the top, and then there's *staying* there. One way to achieve this is to be easy to work *with*. At first, this strategy may seen fundamental, but you'd be surprised to know how many people become arrogant, unpredictable, abusive, self-centered megalomaniacs once they get their first taste of Hollywood success. Or maybe you wouldn't be surprised.

Given that you either have to be a raving egomaniac and/or have a few screws loose just to go into filmmaking in the first place, it's easy to understand why the industry tends to attract "difficult" individuals. Anyone who thinks he has a story that's worth spending $50 million or more to tell, who believes his vision is so compelling that tens of millions of people worldwide will be eager to give up $8 and two hours of their lives to share it, who has the guts and confidence to command an army of thousands and create an entire world from the ground up, is not likely to be a paragon of humility and self-restraint. In fact, with both the stakes and the egos being as vast as they are in the film business, it's a miracle that everyone in Hollywood hasn't already killed each other several times over.

It doesn't help that so many "difficult" stars, producers and directors have been celebrated over the years that one almost feels compelled to follow in their notorious footsteps. From the earliest days of the movies, filmmakers like D.W. Griffith, Erich Von Stroheim and Otto Preminger were lauded not only for their artistic perfectionism, but also for their caustic personalities, their volatile tempers, and their

unfailing belief in their own infallibility. Likewise, the first genera-
tion of studio moguls – titans like Louis B. Mayer, Harry Cohn,
Samuel Goldwyn, and Adolph Zukor – were all infamous for their
explosive tirades and total disregard for social graces. Today, stars
(Roseanne), producers (Joel Silver), writers (Joe Eszterhas) and
directors (James Cameron) are all infamous for being demanding,
temperamental, ego-driven and just plain bullheaded.

Hollywood itself makes no apologies for these personality types.
In fact, the character of the wild, egomaniacal filmmaker/studio
exec has been canonized in such recent films as *Grand Canyon, The
Player, Swimming with Sharks, Mistress* and *An Alan Smithee Film:
Burn Hollywood Burn.* With boorishness being presented as the
norm, how can you *not* believe that this is the way you're supposed
to behave?

Pity the poor filmmaker who actually believes this. We can tell you
of one budding young writer who recently took churlishness to
extremes. After years of writing spec after spec, he'd finally gotten
signed by a major agency, paid a fat advance to do a rewrite for one
studio, and had been offered $200,000 to do a rewrite for another.
Then, in the course of one week, he embezzled hundreds of dollars
from his manager, brazenly declared that he would not do the first
rewrite, refused to return his advance...and then completely dropped
out of sight. Needless to say, the second $200,000 assignment imme-
diately dried up. When asked about the writer's fate, his agent
replied, "Frankly, I don't care if we ever hear from him again."

Strange as it seems, if said writer had been better established he
might have actually gotten away with this bizarre, downright criminal
behavior. (In the 1970s, Columbia Studios Chief David Begelman
embezzled tens of thousands of dollars, got a production deal, and still
had a lengthy career ahead of him.) But pulling such crap right out of
the starting gate is akin to being hired as a part-time secretary and
immediately demanding a company car and keys to the executive
washroom. When you've just gotten your foot in the door, you don't
want to swing it into your host's face.

And you don't have to commit felonies to get on someone's shit list, either. Just refusing to do what you're asked can be enough. Many a writer and director has been fired from a project simply because he/she wouldn't make the changes a producer or studio had demanded. Sometimes this bullheadedness is the result of genuine artistic objections – other times it's simply pure, unadulterated ego. In either case, a massive loss of income and prestige is usually the price one pays for a bit of personal satisfaction.

As a fledging filmmaker, how can you keep the seas around you as smooth as possible? Here are some suggestions:

Be dependable. By definition, a "flake" is someone who's chronically late, who makes plans and then cancels them, who gives all kinds of assurances and then fails to follow through, and who fails to live up to his agreements. Thou shalt not be a flake. You will show up to meetings on schedule. If, for reasons beyond your control, you're going to be late, you'll call ahead and alert the people who are waiting for you. You don't keep shifting appointments around. If, for some pressing reason, you must move a meeting to another date, you will *apologize* for any inconvenience you may have caused. If you promise to have work completed by a certain date, you will, in fact, deliver that work on schedule. You will endeavor to fulfill all aspects of your contract to your employer's satisfaction.

In the real world, this kind of behavior is called "professionalism." In Hollywood, it's called "refreshing."

Listen to notes from your superiors. Everyone, even A-list producers and directors, has to take criticism and "suggestions" at one time or another. A key to surviving in the Hollywood jungle is to give consideration to these comments, especially when they come from people in superior positions, and even when those people are full of shit – which is often.

For creative types, having to kowtow to assembly line studio wonks can be a difficult and sometimes painful task. We each come to a project with a definitive "vision" of what our movie is ideally supposed to be, and when someone in a $3,000 Armani suit who doesn't know a plot point from a ballpoint saunters in and tells us that what our tormented alcoholic really needs is a chimpanzee sidekick, we understandably feel compelled to remove his liver with an apple corer. One must smile inwardly, and suppress such urges.

The first thing you have to realize is that, despite outward appearances to the contrary, most studio executives are *not* idiots. They may sometimes make foolish decisions, have craven ideas, and make ridiculous pronouncements. But, as a rule, they tend to be highly educated, well-informed men and women who genuinely *want* to make good movies. They didn't get to their positions of authority by screwing up worthy stories and producing an endless stream of failures, so it behooves you to give them some respect and honestly listen to what they have to say. Some of their ideas may actually be good. After all, these guys were clever enough to buy *your* project, weren't they?

Next, when dealing with development executives – those men and women on the middle rungs of the studio hierarchy responsible for molding a screenplay into producable form – understand that they are *paid* to make suggestions. It's their job. Even if a screenplay arrived in flawless, shooting-draft condition, they would be obligated to give notes. Pages and pages and pages of notes. If they didn't give notes, if they said a script was perfect as is, they'd be considered slackers and likely get passed over in the next round of promotions, if not fired outright. So recognize that a lot of the notes you'll receive are just so much filler, and learn to take them in stride. There hasn't been a screenplay yet that couldn't be improved, and many of the suggestions you receive may – surprise, surprise – actually be beneficial. The others you can choose to ignore – they'll never notice anyway. (They're too busy giving notes on the *next* project.)

Third, accept the fact that you are a paid *employee*. When you take a studio's money, you forfeit a large degree of personal freedom in return. The only way to have total control over your movie is to raise your own funds. Then you're the boss. Otherwise, be prepared to take orders – or quit.

Fourth, understand that, in addition to being an employee, you're also infinitely expendable. In Hollywood, writers are replaced as regularly as oil filters. Uncooperative producers are routinely bought off and relegated to "consultant" status. Even the all-powerful director is not invincible. When a shoot is not going as planned, studios have been known to change horses midstream. In short, intransigence in the face of overwhelming studio firepower is pointless. To quote *Star Trek*'s implacable Borg, "Resistance is futile."

Stay positive. The best way to stay in good stead with your corporate overlords is to either be silent *or* agree with everything they say, to compliment their intelligence and creativity, and then offer superior ideas of your own. This is called the "Yes, but..." approach.

A filmmaker using the "Yes, but..." may engage in a similar dialogue to this:

Executive: "Could the female hero be a guy?"

Filmmaker: "Yes, but keeping her female helps us avoid all those macho action movie cliches. Plus, it'll give us a great poster."

Executive: "How about moving the climax from New York to Paris? We could have the final battle on the top of the Eiffel Tower, right?"

Filmmaker: "Yes, but staying in New York preserves the story's sense of place. It's our 'arena,' like the office building in *Die Hard*. Plus, staying in one place will save you money, which you can invest in a bigger star."

If an executive insists that you make a change, your next move is to promise to "try" his approach. Later, when his idea fails to appear in your screenplay and/or finished film, you need only explain that you "tried" his suggestion, but it didn't work and this is why. Nine times out of ten, he'll be perfectly satisfied with this.

For example, let's say you're developing a screenplay about a guy who's unwittingly programmed to assassinate a powerful United States Senator. A development executive suggests that, just before the scheduled assassination, the hero should fly off to Las Vegas for a weekend of gambling, drinking and wanton sex. You feel that such an interlude would destroy the rhythm that has been created up to this point, that it's not in the hero's character to engage in such debauchery, and that such a sequence serves no compelling narrative purpose. Do you come out and tell the executive that his idea sucks, that he's a dimwit for even suggesting such a thing, and that, while you're on the subject, you really hate his tie? Not if you want to stay on the project, you don't.

What you say is, "Vegas, huh? That's a really interesting idea, there's a lot you can do in Vegas. The city is incredibly cinematic. And you can't go wrong with a righteous sex scene. Thanks for the suggestion, we'll try to work it in." Two weeks later, you come back and say, "You know, we really loved your Vegas idea, but we just couldn't make it work. We tried to fit it in a dozen different ways, but it always slowed down the story's pacing."

And you know what? At this point, the exec will have forgotten he even made the suggestion in the first place. For you see, many of the "notes" you'll receive during development are off-the-cuff and not completely thought out anyway. They're ideas, possibilities, and "What if's?" The people who make them aren't wedded to them. What they want more than anything is to be heard and acknowledged. Do them this honor and you'll be surprised at how smoothly things will run.

Also, be aware that every suggestion made is fundamentally about broadening the story's appeal – i.e., making more money. The most absurd ideas thrown your way make more sense when the exec's viewpoint is considered. It's about making money, nothing else. When you're expecting this, you can control your outraged laughter and nod thoughtfully.

<u>Appreciate your own power</u>. As a writer, producer or director, you're automatically vested with a high degree of power and influence. As much as studio executives want you to listen to them, they also want to listen to *you*. They're not paying you hundreds of thousands of dollars to take dictation. No, they want you – they *expect* you – to contribute your own ideas and fight for what you believe.

In fact, the more money a studio pays you, the more they expect you to fight for your own positions. If they're paying you a quarter of a million dollars, they figure you must be worth it. So at the same time you're acknowledging the studio's wisdom and promising to take all of their suggestions into consideration, don't hesitate to step forward and offer suggestions of your own. Give 'em their money's worth.

Choose your battles. Chances are, you and your collaborators will come to numerous impasses during the development, production and postproduction processes. You'll want to do things one way; they'll want to do things another. To come out of this with minimal scars, learn to pick your battles wisely. Don't try to win every fight. Instead, acquiesce on those issues of relatively minor importance, and prepare to stand firm on those issues you absolutely, truly believe in. In fact, the best way to make sure that you win on the big issues is to capitulate on the small ones, thus building up an "account" of favors you can cash in when the time is right. "Hey, I gave in to you on A, B and C," you can say. "Now I want D, and I've earned it. You owe me." If your superiors have any sense of justice and fair play, you'll have things your way.

Always remember: it's only a movie. In the heat of the filmmaking process, it's easy to imagine that the Fate of Civilization As We Know It rests on whether or not you get to keep a certain joke in your script or the actor you want is cast in a key role. Well, get over it. In the end, all you're doing is making a movie, a piece of disposable entertainment. The final product may move people, inspire them, make them laugh or cry – but no one's life is riding on its success, and chances are it will be forgotten within five years after its release. As the saying goes, "It ain't brain surgery."

(We're reminded of a recent *New Yorker* cartoon in which two doctors are, in fact, in the midst of brain surgery. One says to the other, "Calm down. It ain't like we're making a movie.")

So, when worse comes to worst, try to set your ego aside and put things in perspective. You're getting paid more money than most people make in a lifetime to have fun and play with what Orson Welles once called "The world's biggest electric train set." Go home. Feed your pet. Mow your lawn. Play with your kids. Have a life.

Your movie may never turn out as you wanted – what ever does? If you've done your best, acted professionally, deferred where deference was due and managed not to piss off too many people along the way, you'll probably get a chance to do it all over again.

And isn't that what a career is all about?

HOLLYWOOD RULE #25: HOW TO TAKE A PLUNGER UP THE ASS, AND OTHER WAYS TO DEAL WITH GETTING SCREWED

Central to the Hollywood filmmaking experience is getting screwed. Not only is it inevitable that you will be screwed sometime during your career; chances are you will be screwed early, often, and with great vigor. There isn't a working producer, director, screenwriter, actor, editor, scenic designer, cinematographer, or clapper loader who doesn't have a mental file brimming with detailed accounts of how he or she's been *shtupped* up one side and down the other, top to bottom, seven ways to Sunday. In fact, there's so much screwing going on in Hollywood that one would think everyone has stock in the Trojan Co.

Your screwing will come in many forms. One is the Broken Promise. You will be told you have a job, you're getting a deal, or some other long-anticipated windfall is about to come your way. You'll wait and wait and wait. At some point you may grow so tired of waiting that you'll become A Pest and demand to know when your Promise is going to be fulfilled. It's at this point you will discover that you didn't get the deal you were promised. It could be that the promise was made with the best of intentions, but the person who made the promise really wasn't in a position to follow through on it. Or the promise may have been a carrot, something to entice you to do something. Perhaps the promise was fulfilled just so you'd be placated for the short-term, to keep you from hounding the promiser – about something else. Regardless of the motive, the result is the same. *You're screwed!*

Another type of screwing is financial. This is perhaps the most popular form of unasked-for fornication in the entertainment industry. The way it works is simple: You work and work and work, and then you never see a dime. (Okay, you may see a dime, but by the time your agent, manager, entertainment lawyer and accountant get through with it, it ain't worth a wooden nickel.)

One of the most popular devices for inflicting this type of penetration is "profit participation." No doubt you've heard stories about a writer, actor, or other creative contributor who was promised a piece of the profits only to see the project end up in the red despite making enough money to sink a battleship. For example, in the 1980s, actor James Garner sued Universal Pictures for what he believed was his promised share of profits generated by his mondo-successful TV series *The Rockford Files*. Universal claimed that, despite a healthy six-year run and ongoing life in syndication, the series lost money. (They eventually settled out of court.) Author Winston Groom, who wrote the original novel *Forrest Gump*, was publicly outraged when told by Paramount Studios that the multi-Oscar-winning movie – which grossed more than $330 million domestically – was still tens of millions of dollars in the red. Actor Dustin Hoffman had a similar public dispute with MGM/UA over his take of the profits generated by the Academy Award-winning blockbuster *Rain Man*.

Such tales are so abundant that the whole concept of "profit participation" has gained the pejorative nickname "monkey points." The implication is that you have to have the IQ of a monkey to believe these "points" in the movie's profits are actually worth anything.

An even more accurate translation: *You're screwed!*

Financial screwing can come from other avenues as well. In addition to being denied a piece of the profits which magically never materialize (you wonder how studios stay in business), you can also be shortchanged when it comes to monies generated by video sales, foreign releases, cable and pay-per-view contracts, and sequels and TV adaptations. It's because of their ability to keep money out of the hands of those people who've earned it that studio accountants have acquired their reputation as "The Most Creative People in Show Business."

Of course, you always have the option of hiring a small army of your *own* accountants to get your due, but such services cost money – *lots* of money. Which means that, even if you're successful, you'll still see only a few cents on each dollar you're owed.

In other words, *Screwed!*

Contrary to popular wisdom, plagiarism – the wholesale theft of entire screenplays – is not a widespread problem in Hollywood. Producers and studios are rarely that blatant. No, it's far easier – and less risky – for people to "borrow" other people's *ideas*, which are much harder to protect. Every time you go into a pitch meeting, you run the risk that the person you're talking to will reject your proposal, only to turn around and sell the idea himself as his own. Such "borrowing" is reported frequently in television, where producers have an enormous amount of time they *must* fill, and where writers can quickly run out of fresh new ideas of their own, especially on series that have already run for several seasons.

(In their defense, TV producers tend to hear the same types of pitches over and over again from freelance writers. When an idea is bought, there are always dozens of other people who claim to have had the same or a similar concept. And this may, in fact, be the case. But there's no way to pay and credit *everyone* who's come up with the pitch "Character A and Character B get stuck in an elevator." So the practice remains.)

Although most writers, producers and directors don't conduct meetings with the express purpose of stealing other people's stories, it's impossible not to be influenced by ideas hurled at you fourteen hours every day. Something someone said to you today, yesterday, or two years ago is bound to creep into your thinking, even subconsciously, as you struggle to develop ideas of your own. And if you're the person who gave that other writer, producer or director an idea that eventually made its way into his multimillion dollar opus, do you think you can successfully make a claim on it? Forget it. Ha! *Screwed again!*

Writers, almost by tradition, are screwed by getting bounced off the projects they initiated. Often, you won't even be told you've been fired. You'll just never get a reaction to your latest draft. It's only when you read in the trades that your film has gone into production – and you're not even listed on the credits – that you know you've just taken it up the pooper.

Writers must also routinely suffer the indignity of Writers Guild arbitration. When more than one writer has worked on a film, the WGA mandates that *they* determine who will get the final credit. If you wrote the original screenplay, only to have it completely rewritten by some hack, you may only end up with a "Story by" credit – if any at all. On the other hand, *you* could completely rewrite an inferior piece of work, replacing all of the original writer's leaden dialogue with your own sparkling badinage, but because the WGA doesn't consider dialogue to be a substantial contribution, you end up with no credit at all. More than mere ego gratification is at stake here. More often than not, final remuneration is contingent on actually having your name on the movie. So either way the arbitration goes, you can be royally...screwed!

If you're a producer, you can be screwed in any number of delightfully wicked ways. The simplest is to simply be ignored once a more powerful producer is brought on board. You may have been the one to have found the screenplay, you may have helped the writer polish it to perfection, you may have set it up at the studio and even have found the director. But if you don't yet have a sterling track record or another form of negotiable clout, it's Fuck-O-Rama, baby!

Because of their power – both real and imagined – directors are more resistant than others to unsolicited anal violation. But they're hardly immune. Although a director is usually Top Dog during pre-production and the actual shoot, once a film is in the can, it can be anybody's game. This is particularly true when it comes to the all-important "final cut." It's not unusual for a studio or its producers to seize control of a film after a director has done the first editing pass and then reassemble it – in some cases, outright "butcher" it – to suit *their* vision. A director may then be saddled with an inferior film for which he may be unjustly blamed.

(The Director's Guild of America has an odd method for dealing with this situation. If a director doesn't approve of the finished product, he may pull his name off the picture and have it replaced with the all-purpose pseudonym "Alan Smithee." The most notorious "Alan Smithee" film is 1998's so-called "Hollywood satire" *An Alan Smithee Film*, written by infamous *Showgirls* scribe Joe Eszterhas. Although meant to satirize bad movies, it turned out to be so unwatchable itself that the director, *Love Story*'s Arthur Hiller, had his name replaced with the pseudonym. The prophecy of the title was neatly fulfilled, and no one got screwed but the ten or so people who actually sat through the thing.)

Of course, removing your name from a project doesn't make the experience any more pleasant. There may be less public humiliation, but everyone in town still knows what happened, and you still have to write off the last year or two of your life. In other words, *Screw City, USA!*

Knowing that you're going to be spending much of your professional life grabbing your ankles, the question is: How does one deal? Do you assemble an army of lawyers and publicists and fight every indignation, theft and injustice with all legal means at your disposal?

Hell, no.

As we've stated earlier, Hollywood is a town built on *relationships.* If you attack everyone you think has done you wrong, it won't be long before you don't have a friend west of the San Andreas Fault. And without friends (at least the Hollywood definition thereof), you won't get work. As the saying goes, if you want to get along, go along. As much as anything, this refers to taking whatever perversions they dish out to you, and taking it with a smile.

Is this easy? No. More than once in your career you will you have the urge to fire off a nasty letter or yell at someone over the phone or call your lawyer or smash someone's windshield with a sledgehammer. You must *resist.* Such explosions may be divinely cathartic, but they won't lead to a new contract. In fact, it'll help you develop the reputation of one who is "difficult," "litigious," or perhaps even "psychotic." Either way, you'll become a pariah. And you'll never work in this town again.

So buck up, spread those cheeks, and set your sights on the horizon. Take that old unvarnished plunger up the wazoo enough times and, who knows, it may be *you* doing the screwing one day.

Ah, to graduate from *screwee* to *screwer* – ain't Hollywood grand?

HOLLYWOOD RULE #26: SHARE THE CREDIT

A Hollywood tradition that all America loves to mock is the Academy Awards acceptance speech. Every March, over two dozen filmmaking professionals – some famous, some obscure – stride up to the podium, receive their glittering gold statuettes, and spend the next thirty seconds thanking the Academy voters, their agents, their second-grade kung-fu instructors, and all the other "little people" who helped make the coveted win possible. Of the billion-or-so viewers the Academy purports watch this glitzfest annually, at least 99 percent consider such gushing gratitude to be yet one more example of Hollywood insincerity. The public knows that if – like Jim Carrey in *Liar, Liar* – these Tinseltown phonies were magically compelled to tell the truth, the recipients would no doubt announce, "This is *my* Oscar! *I* earned it! *I* deserve it! And I don't owe nobody nothin', 'cause I did it all *myself!*"

The public couldn't be more wrong.

If there's one thing everyone in Hollywood knows, it's that film-making is a collaborative medium. It takes hundreds, sometimes *thousands* of people to make and market a motion picture. Even writer-producer-actor-directors like Woody Allen, Spike Lee, Albert Brooks and Robert Duvall need an army of technicians, performers, financiers and marketing mavens to help them properly bring their stories to life. Anyone who thinks he can prosper as a one-man-band is not only sorely mistaken, but isn't likely to reach first base in the film industry.

Know that if and when you succeed in this business it will be due to the encouragement, support and invaluable contributions of the people you work with. This is a key reason why we've repeatedly stressed the need to maintain good relationships with everyone, regardless of what you may think of them personally. If you can get people to rally to your cause, if you can motivate others to do their best for *you*, you'll be far more powerful than if you charge into battle armed only with your good looks and ambition.

Of course, you don't have to win an Oscar to express your gratitude to those who've helped boost you up the ladder of success. While you're working, it's always prudent to throw an occasional "Thank you" to people who are doing a good job on behalf of your film. If you're a producer, you want to regularly compliment the creative contributors, technical personnel, and studio folks who are helping to give your movie shape and substance. After all, when people feel appreciated, they tend to go above and beyond the call of duty – sometimes without even getting paid for it! As a director, the best way to maintain a "happy set" is to make sure each person feels wanted, needed and creatively valuable. An occasional "Good job" or "Great idea" can keep energy levels high and creative juices flowing well into Golden Time. And as a writer, you need to acknowledge those people – producers, directors, actors and yes, even *other* writers – for their creative input. This can be difficult for writers, as they tend to be particularly protective of their work and tend to see any changes as bastardization, butchery, and/or full frontal assaults on artistic freedoms everywhere. Hey, writers, loosen up!

Expressions of gratitude are important not only during the creation of a film, but afterwards as well. When discussing a completed film – or basking in the glory of a recent success – it's important to share the credit with your fellow contributors. Only an ass takes all the credit for himself. (And we *do* know a few asses, don't we?)

When receiving compliments on a finished work, be gracious enough to mention the good work the actors did, or the critical contributions of the director of photography, the composer, or the editor. Say good things about your other creative contributors, whether the director, the writers, the producers, or the studio honchos. Let your listener know that you recognize, and value, the talents and hard work of *all* the people who made the movie. Not only does this demonstrate that you have a realistic view of your own place in the Industry continuum, but by expressing your good feelings about other people, you make other people feel good about *you*. Everyone you meet will know that, should they ever be lucky enough to work with you, their contributions will be properly acknowledged.

Now, you may wonder, does this same philosophy apply to *failures*? When commiserating about a film that for whatever reason didn't quite work, do you parcel out blame as easily as you doled out credit?

Absolutely *not*.

First, you don't want to go around bad-mouthing other movie people. Cardinal Sin numero uno in Hollywood. Just like doctors, lawyers, and Republicans never speak ill of one another for fear of undermining their careers, film folks should say nothing if they can't say something nice. Hell, we already have enough detractors without *you* making things worse. On a more personal level, if you start spewing venom about some producer, director, writer, or studio exec you feel botched his job, word of such criticism will no doubt get back to that person and he will, in turn, bad-mouth *you*. This is how bad reputations get started.

Just as there's no way to credit any one person for a movie's success, no single individual is ever truly responsible for a film's failure. No one ever sets out to make a bad movie. Everyone does his or her best within the time and budget restraints of a given production. When a movie crashes and burns, it can be due to everything from a difficult story premise to faulty casting to choppy editing to an ill-conceived marketing plan. Usually, it's a combination of myriad factors.

Instead of trying to lay the blame on a single individual, you're better off just saying something to the effect of "Hey, sometimes the magic works and sometimes it doesn't," and letting it go at that. We've all had our share of failures as well as successes, and we're all smart enough to know that if anyone *really* knew how to make sure-fire hits, that genius would be richer than Steven Spielberg, James Cameron, Tom Cruise and Jerry Bruckheimer *combined.*

So be generous with your praise and miserly with your criticism. What goes around comes around – you might as well make it something nice.

HOLLYWOOD RULE #27: TAKE THE MONEY AND (DON'T WALK) RUN

In our last chapter, we discussed the wisdom of sharing credit and diffusing blame. There's a corollary to this *Hollywood Rule* that applies primarily to writers, but can also serve anyone whose creative input is subject to change by others. The rule is simple: Take the money and make a mad dash for your financial institution.

Writers are infamous for their tendency to bitch and whine about how their scripts have been raped by the talentless Philistines who are ultimately responsible for a film's final form. And to a large extent, their vitriol is justified. There probably hasn't been a film made in the last fifty years that is a totally faithful rendering of the writer's original vision. More often than not, a "spec" script that gets purchased is rewritten and rewritten again long before the first frame of film is exposed. Sometimes the original writer, working in conjunction with the director and/or various studio executives makes these revisions. Sometimes the original writer is bounced unceremoniously off his own film, only to be rewritten by one (or ten or twenty) replacements. The resulting script may or may not bear even a faint resemblance to the one that first caught the studio's attention.

Sometimes the results of such musical-chair-rewrites can be good, and sometimes they're bad. For example, 1982's *Tootsie* – a critical and commercial smash – was rewritten repeatedly by a cadre of writers, not just the three who ultimately received screenplay credit. At the other end of the spectrum, over forty writers reportedly worked on 1994's *The Flintstones*, resulting in a silly, hackneyed mess. But regardless of the outcome, it's always difficult for the *original* writer not to believe that he has not somehow been compromised for the sake of commerce.

Of course, screenwriters aren't the only ones who invariably see their works mutated during the development process. Best-selling novelists like Stephen King, Tom Clancy, Michael Crichton, and John Grisham must routinely endure the indignity of seeing their beloved books gutted as various Hollywood hacks struggle to adapt them for the cinema, and these are the Big Boys. What lesser-known authors must suffer. Lauded playwrights like Neil Simon, Arthur Miller and David Mamet, men who enjoy unquestioned veto power on their home turf, are powerless to keep their "children" from being eviscerated when they're sold into the Tinseltown factory. Even William Shakespeare, The Bard himself, is not spared a little creative tinkering. In fact, Shakespeare adaptations have traditionally carried "screenwriter" credits to honor those who have made these hallowed 400-year-old works "suitable" for the silver screen.

As we noted earlier, movies can be massacred even after they're shot. Poor editing can turn a rich, moving narrative into an incomprehensible nightmare, prompting the director to resort to the good old "Alan Smithee" pseudonym. Producers can be shunted aside by more powerful filmmakers who are brought onto a project midway through their gestation, resulting in vastly diminished control. In such cases, producers and directors have just as much reason to be outraged as writers, right?

Well, just because you *can* be doesn't mean you *should*. Just because you *can* drink a six-pack and drive your car down the freeway at 90 MPH doesn't make it a good idea. And just because you may be fully justified in complaining about how badly your work has been butchered doesn't make such beefing desirable, at least not in earshot of anyone else.

To survive in Hollywood, you have to accept the fact that, with scant few exceptions, *nobody* gets things their way. Everybody compromises, and is compromised. In this sense, Hollywood is a lot like Washington, D.C. The only way things get done is by taking a good idea and then bending, twisting, cutting and gutting it until it contains something that everyone likes and nothing that anyone really hates. As Sir Winston Churchill remarked about democracy, this may be the most wasteful and inefficient system in the world, but it's still the best.

And as with the democratic process, the Hollywood system is not without its rewards: people get paid very well for putting up with bull-shit. *Very* well. Today, the average studio screenplay sells for over $300,000. Even a writer who's tossed overboard after his first rewrite can walk away with more money than most Americans make in five years of hard labor. Directors, producers and other creative folk likewise reap enormous financial benefits for their willingness to play the Hollywood game.

But does obscene financial remuneration buy silence? Aren't people who compromise their artistic integrity for money nothing more than whores? That's certainly one way to look at it. Another way is to realize that the studio didn't tell you how to spend your money when it paid *you*, so you have no right to tell it what to do with your project after you've sold it to *them*. It doesn't matter that you "created" a story. The guy who designed your car can't tell you how to maintain it. An architect can't decree how you paint or furnish your house. Once you buy something, you *own* it; it's yours to do with as you see fit. This same dictum applies to screenplays and finished films.

So kick back, loosen up, and enjoy what satisfaction you *can* derive from your work. Always remember that there are millions of people the world over who would just *love* the opportunity to "sell out" to Hollywood. Be grateful for the moment when that opportunity is yours.

HOLLYWOOD RULE #28: PACE YOURSELF

Breaking into movies is hard work. Staying in the industry can be just as difficult. Just as the music business is filled with one-hit wonders – performers who exploded into the Top 10 and were never heard from again – so is the history of filmmaking awash in writers, producers and directors who had one or two hits, then vanished off the Hollywood radar. The attrition rate among writers is particularly severe. A good many scribes sell scripts that, for reasons beyond their control, never get made, and their careers stall. There are some writers who write a single megahit – and maybe even win an Oscar for their efforts – but who never again taste success. And then there are those filmmakers – producers and directors as well as writers – who squander their sudden good fortune on high living. They spend, snort, and screw themselves right into oblivion.

It's easy to understand how sudden success can be as difficult to manage as prolonged failure. Because they've struggled for so long to make it, people who do finally hit the Hollywood jackpot are naturally tempted to take every offer that comes their way, regardless of quality or personal suitability. They may commit themselves to a half-dozen projects, at an equal number of studios without regard for the time or effort required to fulfill these contracts. Some overnight successes experience critical ego overload.

They begin to see themselves as stars or auteurs before their first project is even put into production, and make untenable financial and/or creative demands on their studios. (Recently, a young indie director, having signed on for his first low-budget studio project, demonstrated his celebrated talent for guerrilla filmmaking by demanding, among other luxuries, six first-class airline tickets for his casting director. The studio was not amused.) On a personal level, years of hardship can create an appetite for The Good Life that seizes control of one's will and sends one into an orgy of wild spending, promiscuous sex, and various mind-altering pharmaceuticals. The results can often be disastrous.

(More than one Flavor of the Month has burned himself out on drugs and alcohol, or spent himself into bankruptcy. We know one writer who sold his first spec for a modest $150,000, then immediately proceeded to reward himself with a $75,000 Ferrari. He hasn't worked since...but does drive a nice car.)

The trick to surviving success is to *pace yourself.* Take things slowly and in moderation. Don't expect to become Steven Spielberg overnight, or to move from a one-bedroom apartment in Santa Monica straight into a mansion in Beverly Hills. Be as disciplined with your life as you are with your work.

When it comes to money, never spend what you don't yet have. Just because you make a deal doesn't mean you actually have cash. Not long ago, a writer we know sold a made-for-TV movie to a network's in-house production company. Two weeks later, the company was disbanded. Although a deal memo had been signed, there hadn't even been time to draw up contracts. The deal dissolved. In another case, a hot young director was signed to helm a moderately budgeted feature film. Then an A-list star was brought on, the budget quadrupled, and the director was fired in favor of a famous hit-maker. Since it wasn't a pay-or-play situation, the director was screwed.

An independent producer we know was owed nearly $50,000 by a major production company which insisted that her so-called minimal input negated her getting her full fee on a project she herself had originated. (Oh, she'd tried to input plenty, but the production company's A-list players had frozen her out.) She had to threaten a lawsuit in order to get the money due to her.

The list of such Hollywood Horror Stories is endless, but the moral is always the same: It ain't yours 'til it's yours.

And even when you *do* get your big bucks, the bucks are not *all* yours. Uncle Sam is gonna want his share. So will the Governor. Not to mention your lawyer, your accountant, and everyone else in your camp.

How much? Well, let's have fun and pretend you've just made $1 million. (Whoopee!) First, your agent will take 10 percent off the top; that leaves you with $900,000. If you have a manager, he/she will take another 10-15 percent of the original $1 million. That's $150,000, leaving you with $750,000. Many entertainment lawyers have deals which stipulate that they will work unlimited hours regarding a project for 5 percent (10 percent without an agent) of your gross. So whack off another $50,000, which leaves you with $700,000. Getting queasy? Wait! There's more! Now the IRS and the Franchise Tax Board will want their cuts. Fortunately, they're only entitled to take the money you've earned *after* expenses, so they'll only be pecking at the $700,000...to the tune of about 45 percent (state and federal combined). So, in the end, what began as a cool million has been reduced to a mere $400,000. Sure, you get some deductions, but how much debt do you owe, and how many years have you put in? Not quite the windfall you imagined, is it? (Awwwwww.)

Now, there are ways to minimize this drain. If you didn't have a manager, you could save 10-15 percent right off the top. And if your attorney works on an hourly basis – and he doesn't have to work too many hours – you might be able to get away with paying him/her only $5,000-$10,000 instead of the $50,000 in this example.

But even if your expenses are minimal, the tax bite is still going to be immense. Whatever you make, put away at least half for taxes. A smart bet many newcomers should acquire: a business manager. An entertainment accountant should be able to reduce that tax burden somewhat and initiate a money-saving strategy (i.e., incorporation) to keep your pockets full. When it comes to dealing with the IRS, it's always better to be safe than very, very sorry.

(Just ask Jerry Lee Lewis and Willie Nelson.)

Assuming you got your money and paid your taxes, what should you spend your money *on*? A big house? A fast car? Probably not. The one guarantee in show business is that there *are* no guarantees, and one success doesn't necessarily lead to another. Like the guy who bought the $75,000 Ferrari and never worked again, free spending could leave you in a worse position than you were in *before* you made your deal. The wise filmmaker waits until his or her *second* success to start spending the money from the first. After all, one deal does not a career make, and only by tracking your income over the long term can you determine what you can and cannot afford.

You must also pace yourself when it comes to professionally exploiting your sudden fame and fortune. It's said that nothing succeeds like success, and in Hollywood, this is more the case than anywhere. Someone who's a virtual unknown will suddenly be everyone's best friend when the news of a major deal appears in the trades. Offers will rush in from all corners, many of which will carry attractive price tags but god-awful content. *Resist temptation.* Don't grab at the first offer that comes along. Take your time. Be picky. Remember, the one thing you want to avoid is Sophomore Slump: the dreaded tendency to perform below expectations your second time out. Find a project you *really* believe in, something that you'd enjoy working on even if you didn't get paid (God forbid).

At the same time, you mustn't let fear of falling short your second time out paralyze you. Very often, creative people are so afraid that their first success was just a fluke – that they'll never again be able to capture that lightning in a bottle – that they avoid the possibility of a follow-up failure by simply doing nothing. This lack of movement is just as dangerous as moving too hastily. Being chronically myopic, studio execs can only see objects in motion; if you're standing still, they'll forget you're even there. To use a baseball metaphor: wait for your pitch, then swing for the bleachers. Never let yourself be called out on strikes.

Vaulting ambition is another problem area for many Overnight Successes. Writers immediately want to direct. Producers want their own production companies. Directors resurrect some pet project that's been gathering dust since junior high school and foist it on a studio, along with a $100 million price tag. The results of such excesses are rarely pretty.

The irony, of course, is that there *was* a time when the Too Much-Too Soon Syndrome was a rarity. Back in the glory days of the old Studio System, careers were managed by powerful moguls who groomed up-and-coming talent over the course of many films. Back in the Olden Days, a director might start by making two-reel comedies. After a year or two of this, if the director showed promise, he might be promoted to directing programmers, the fast-and-cheap B-movies that usually filled the second half of double features, which studios churned out like today's TV shows. Since the shooting schedules of such films rarely lasted more than just a few weeks, a director might have a good dozen of these potboilers under his belt before he finally made it to the Big Show – the A-picture, where he got to work with decent budgets and top name stars. Even then, it was usually the studio bosses who called the shots. Producers and directors might be egotistical and temperamental, but most understood the necessity of surviving within the highly structured commercial operation that was the Hollywood picture factory of old.

But like Big Bands, nickel candy bars, and polio, the idea of the slow-but-steady career ascent is long gone, at least in the motion picture business. We're in the era of Instant Gratification, where first-time writers expect – and often get – $500,000 paydays, and directors proceed right from directing thirty-second commercials and three-minute music videos to helming $80 million action movies with Bruce Willis, Nicolas Cage and Sean Connery. The temptation is to exploit sudden success for all it's worth. Hey, it could disappear overnight, right? Git while the gittin's good!

Once success hits, a producer can set up projects at studios, a writer can get hired to do $100,000-a-week rewrites, a director can do $1 million commercials – a means to maintain the flash new lifestyle, sure. But also a distraction from what we're all really here to do: make movies.

Followers of the *Hollywood Rules* know better. You recognize that talent is important, but that there's no teacher like experience. You grab only for that which is within your reach, and wisely acknowledge your own limitations. You're able to look *beyond* the moment or the project at hand, and consider your career in the *long term*. Like Aesop's turtle, you know that slow and steady wins the race.

And when the other hotshots burn out like so many meteoric flashes-in-the-pan, you will continue to shine.

HOLLYWOOD RULE #29: KEEP THE KARMA GODS HAPPY – OR ELSE!

We've spent the last twenty-eight chapters providing you with specific, time-tested guidelines for establishing and nurturing a career as a

Hollywood filmmaker. We've given you lists of do's and don'ts designed to bolster your professional credibility, and to help you overcome the obstacles that stand in the way of anyone attempting to break into the movie business. But the reality is that you can accumulate all of the technical skills in the world, have talent up the yin-yang, work like a son-of-a-bitch, make all the right connections, live in the right neighborhood, wear the right clothes, drive the right car, eat at the right restaurants, exude the charm of a master politician, and still go nowhere in this town if you lack one absolutely critical ingredient: *Luck*.

It's said that Napoleon Bonaparte once rejected a brilliant general for a key battlefield position because of the man's prolonged lack of good fortune. "I don't want a general who's smart, I want one who's *lucky!*" Napoleon reportedly snarled (in French, of course). Likewise, there are plenty of brilliant, educated and skilled writers, producers and directors who have been stumbling around Hollywood for years with nothing to show for their efforts because of their lack of *simple dumb luck*. There's the producer who was all set to roll on a $5 million independent film when his benefactor, a self-made millionaire, dropped dead. There's the writer whose scripts always got great coverage, but whose stories were always too similar to *other* stories the production companies had already purchased earlier. There's the director whose first few films received critical accolades, but which were released head-to-head against bigger, splashier, super-hyped megahits. They – like so many filmmakers just like them – are still waiting for their ever-elusive big breaks.

The luck factor is so formidable in Hollywood that Industry folk are notorious for being some of the most superstitious people in the world. Otherwise well read, well-traveled, college-educated filmmakers regularly consult astrologers or tarot readers. There's many an actor or director who won't step on a movie set without some kind of lucky charm. More than a few Academy Award-nominees have worn tattered underwear or mismatched socks just because they're considered lucky. It's no wonder the number of followers of Kabbalah, the Forum and Scientology are all larger in Los Angeles than anywhere else on earth!

Of course, some are more pragmatic. They believe that successful people make their *own* luck. To a certain extent, they do: by knowing what you want, knowing how to get it, and then aggressively doing what you must do to realize those goals you can certainly turn the odds in your favor. That's why you're reading the *Hollywood Rules*.

But at the same time, happenstance does usually play a key role in peoples' lives. No more so than in Hollywood, where – as William Goldman so aptly put it in his seminal autobiography *Adventures in the Screen Trade* – "Nobody knows anything." Anyone who thinks he or she can get a movie made by nothing but sheer force of will is a fool of the highest order.

So, the question becomes, is there any way to turn divine providence in your favor? To help ensure that your fresh romantic comedy will land on the desk of an executive at the precise moment he's looking for a fresh romantic comedy? To make sure that you wind up at the same party as the producer you've been dying to meet? To guarantee that the star you need to make your $100-million action flick will drop out of his $10-million indie project just when you need him?

The only way to address this is to get metaphysical. Regardless of your religious or philosophical background, it helps to consider the idea of Karma; that everything we do in life exerts a power on everything else we do. A more prosaic way of stating this is: What Goes Around Comes Around. If you do good things, good things happen to you. If you do bad things, your life may well become miserable.

God knows, there appear to be numerous exceptions to this rule. We all know of kind, polite, charitable people who love their mothers and have never shoplifted so much as a pack of gum, yet who are constantly beset by problems ranging from corporate downsizing to fatal malignancies. At the same time, we've known or have read about crooks, thieves, murderers and all-around dastardly bastards who live like kings. Our only response here is that a good number of "successful" assholes are actually pretty miserable people who live in constant fear, whose personal lives are often in shambles, and who have a significantly higher incidence of dying prematurely by drug overdoses, bullet wounds, and driving their fancy Ferraris into trees. A lot of them, at the very least, wind up in rehab or prison.

At the same time, while nice guys may sometimes finish last, most are able to sleep at night. They certainly don't have to worry about winding up as Bubba's little bitch or spending Christmas in "the hole."

Although no system is foolproof, it's certainly to your benefit to keep the Karma Gods happy. Behave ethically. When you make a promise, keep it. Don't badmouth others; even your worst enemies. Take responsibility for your actions. Be honest with yourself and with others. If you hurt another person, either by omission or commission, apologize. Give to charity. Do a friend a favor. Do a *stranger* a favor – and *make* a friend. Give a compliment whenever you can. Loan a buddy ten bucks, and don't expect to ever get it back. Smile. Doing favors for Industry people – no matter at what level – can only help your cause.

And *pray*. Even if you're not the least bit religious. Acknowledge that there is a power greater than you are, and throw yourself on its mercy. Why? Because prayer creates hope, and without hope you'll never accomplish what you need to, and get that "lucky" break you've been waiting for.

Now that we think about it, perhaps we *do* make our own luck; but it's not the clear cause-and-effect pattern we seek for in Newtonian physics. Instead of an "If-I-Do-This-I-Get-That" scenario, make a world in which your actions slowly but steadily accumulate over time to create an atmosphere in which good things *can* happen. The more good things we do, the better the odds grow in our favor.

And since we never know which of our actions will have positive results, we have to behave as though *all* our actions have repercussions. So let's fly straight, respect others, and above all, follow the *Hollywood Rules*.

It couldn't hurt, right?

HOLLYWOOD RULE #30: DON'T SHARE THE RULES!

As you've probably gathered by now, Hollywood is an extremely competitive and endlessly complex place. It *is* the Town Without Pity, where Winning *is* the Only Thing, and you're only as good as what you can do for someone *else*. This is not a town for the squeamish, the timid, the faint of heart, or those prone to equivocation. It demands a great deal from a person, and at the same time its rewards are boundless. Filmmakers are veritable gods who can fashion humans in their own image and manipulate them with precision that would make the residents of Mt. Olympus envious. Through flickering images on a great silver screen, we have the power to make people laugh, cry, scream, and perhaps even think. Motion pictures allow us to share our dreams with people of every race, language, religion and nationality in the world and, if we're successful, we can live lives that rival those of foreign royalty.

Very cool, indeed.

When rewards this great are available, however remotely, everyone wants a piece of the action. Thousands of people come to Southern California every year with hopes of becoming the next Steven Spielberg, Spike Lee, or James Cameron. Film schools are filled to capacity, screenwriting seminars consistently sell out, and everyone from your dentist to the geek behind the counter at McDonald's can quote you the weekend box-office grosses. With so much competition, it's difficult for even the most talented among us to attract the kind of attention necessary to get ahead. The odds stacked against any one individual are almost inconceivable.

So we do all we can to tilt the odds in our favor; to level the playing field. We develop our talent. We hone our craft. We study the marketplace. And we follow the *Hollywood Rules* to fortify our credibility and our value to others.

Then, to keep the competition as weak as possible, we keep the *Rules* to ourselves. We guard its wisdom as closely as we would the tenets of a secret society, a top-secret military code, or our checking account PIN number. We endure the envy and occasional wrath of our peers when we make a valuable connection or land a major studio deal; we ascribe our success to experience, perseverance, and good dumb luck. We never so much as hint that they, too, could have a Michael Jordan-sized leg up on the competition by following a few simple rules in a book.

Is this cruel? Selfish? Cynical? Machiavellian? Does this close-to-the-vest approach reek of the kind of I-Got-Mine-So-Up-Yours attitude that has turned many people off to Hollywood altogether?

Perhaps. But we like to think of it as simple self-preservation.

Sharing the *Hollywood Rules* is a bad idea. Revealing them will only ensure that everyone has the same advantages. In such a case, the chances of you getting anywhere become as small as an agent's conscience. Sure, you may feel better about yourself – but only until you read in *The Hollywood Reporter* that the waiter at Starbucks you lent your book to just sold a pitch to Paramount for $300,000.

So be smart. Doing the odd good deed to keep the Karma Gods happy is one thing, but it doesn't extend to shooting yourself in the foot. You have a powerful weapon here; such power needs to be tightly controlled or it may fall into the wrong hands.

Don't share the *Hollywood Rules*. Instead, do the world a *real* favor: make good movies.

OTHER RULES TO LIVE BY

Having lived and worked in Hollywood for far longer than is deemed healthy, we've discovered a number of rules that don't fit neatly into the thirty sections that make up the bulk of this book. Yet these sub-rules are just as valuable as all the other information we've collected, and we'd be remiss if we didn't pass them on to you. Some of them may seem trivial or may only be applicable in a few rare situations. But, like a cute little 9mm tucked into an ankle holster, they might just save your keister in an emergency.

Here then, in no particular order, are some additional *Hollywood Rules* to live by:

• Learn the difference between confidence and arrogance. Confidence is firm but quiet. Arrogance is loud and obnoxious. Confident people inspire trust in the people around them. Arrogant people inspire anger.
• If you're a writer, it's very dangerous to openly admit you want to direct. *Everyone* wants to direct, and to state your ambitions is to invite scorn and ridicule. Although it can be frustrating, your best bet is to write well enough so that you achieve a certain level of success, at which point someone will likely *suggest* that you try your hand behind the camera. At this point, you're in the power position and can dictate your terms.
• If you're discussing your screenplay with someone, always ask how he or she found the *ending*. If they can discuss the end in any detail, chances are they actually read the script.
• When you're meeting someone new, never put out your hand to shake

first. Some people don't like to shake hands; it's a neurotic thing, and Hollywood's a neurotic town. Instead, wait for *them* to reach out to shake hands with *you*.

• The only thing of any value in Hollywood is a *written contract*. "We love it!" means nothing. "Let's do it!" means nothing. "It's a deal!" means nothing. The only time a deal is a deal is when both parties have signed on the dotted line. And even then, you have to wait 'til the check clears.

• Never go into business with someone who asks you to pay him (or her). We recently heard of a "name" producer who asked a novelist to kick in $3,500 to pay for a WGA-credited writer to compose a TV miniseries treatment. Genuine producers don't work this way. If someone says you need to put up-front money just to make a presentation, your red flags should wave like an old-time May Day parade. Likewise, don't submit your material to agencies that charge reader fees, or subject yourself to peer pressure when a noted "guru" asks for $5,000 to help sell your script. Quality agencies don't charge for submissions. And gurus don't charge fees to assist already-paying students in selling their already-salable stories.

• Don't post your ideas on the Internet – no matter who's asking for them. Ideas cannot be copyrighted!!!

• Be wary of agents or producers who talk in huge dollar terms. If someone tells you, "We can sell this book to ABC for $1 million," or "I can get you $500,000 to direct this $5-million movie," you should figure you're dealing with a flake. Know what the going rate for goods and services are in your field, and adjust your expectations accordingly. True, some people *do* hit the jackpot. But the old saying goes, *If something sounds too good to be true, it probably is.*

• If you're up for a job as either a writer or director, always give 'em your best ideas. Don't be afraid that they're going to steal these ideas and then give the job to someone else. If this *does* happen, it's only because they were planning to hire the other guy in the first place. All other things being equal, the only way to get a job is to give it your best shot. You can't impress people with your genius by holding back.

• Always be open to meet on weekends. Although weekend meetings may interfere with your family life or other social plans, they tend to be very productive. People are more relaxed on weekends, and there are far fewer interruptions.

• Always admit it when you don't know something. Nobody knows everything, and it's far better to admit ignorance than to be caught bullshitting. Also, when people discover they know something that you *don't*, it makes them feel good about *themselves* – which in the end is to your benefit.

• Be careful about name-dropping. It's usually considered boorish. Only name-drop when the reference slips neatly into the conversation – even then, it's always nice to apologize for your bad manners. And never refer to famous actors by their nicknames, even if they're actually friends of yours. If you refer to Dustin Hoffman as "Dusty" or Robert De Niro as "Bobby Dee," you're going to look like a pretentious idiot. Just use the names by which they're most commonly known.

• Before turning in a draft of a screenplay to a producer, director, agent or studio, give it to at least three fellow filmmakers – whose objective opinions you trust – for feedback. This important first step can help you stay on a project.

• Never let 'em see you sweat. Nothing is as repulsive in Hollywood as the stench of desperation. Never let slip to someone how much you need a job, how many times your project has been rejected, or how badly a shoot is going. As far as the outside world is concerned, you are the quintessence of cool. Hollywood is so rife with uncertainty that people will immediately latch on to anyone who even *pretends* to know what he's doing.

• Have fun. This is the *entertainment* business, and you'll do a whole lot better at it if you don't take yourself too seriously. Enjoy yourself, enjoy the work, and even enjoy the struggle. When life looks bleak, employ your creative talents and fantasize. Write yourself a new career scenario. And give yourself a happy ending.

In this town, dreams *do* come true.

A GLOSSARY OF HOLLYWOODSPEAK

As in all industries, Hollywood has its own lexicon. To fit in with the pros, you need to be able to understand and utilize the local slang. Here, then, is the *Hollywood Rules* guide to *Hollywoodspeak*:

A-List (noun): A theoretical list of actors, producers, writers, and directors, all of whom are considered strong enough to ensure that a movie gets made, released, and seen in sufficiently large numbers. This list changes weekly, depending on who's hot at any given time. Some filmmakers, like Steven Spielberg and George Lucas, are on the permanent A-list. They can have the occasional *1941* or *Howard the Duck* and everyone in town will still want to be in business with them. Others can make the A-list based on one or two major hits, but will fall to the B-list after one or two flops.

Above the Line (adj.): That part of a movie's budget that covers costs associated with major creative talent: the stars, the director, the producer(s) and the writer(s). In a small, star-driven movie like *As Good as It Gets*, Above-the-line expenditures account for a majority of the film's budget. In big event movies with middle-range stars but huge technical budgets like *Jurassic Park* or *Godzilla*, Above-the-line fees may only be twenty or thirty percent of the film's cost. (*Ant.: Below-The-Line.*)

Act One (noun): The first section of a movie – usually its first quarter – in which characters are introduced, problems established, and the story set in motion. Also known as a story's Set-Up.

Act Two (noun): A film's mid-section, usually its middle hour. The transition from Set-Up to Climax. Scripts traditionally suffer from

Act Two problems, since this is often the longest and least structured part of a screenplay.

Act Three (noun): A film's climax and conclusion. Here, the "hero" and "villain" have their final battle and the situation is resolved for better or worse.

Ancillaries (noun): Venues other than *conventional* theaters where films make money. Currently, ancillary markets include videocassette and DVD/laserdisc sales, pay-per-view, cable, broadcast TV, and airline in-flight showings. In many cases, ancillary revenue may actually *exceed* a movie's theatrical take.

Attach (verb): To get a commitment – either formal or informal – from a major star, writer, producer, or director to work on a film. Sometimes attachments are obtained with actual contracts, but more often than not they're simply verbal agreements.

Auction (noun/verb): To offer a screenplay to several potential buyers simultaneously in hopes of jacking up the price. Script auctions were very popular in the late 1980s and early 1990s, but have since fallen somewhat out of favor.

B-List (noun): Those actors and filmmakers who are on their way up, on their way down, or who are perennial also-rans. The B-list also includes niche filmmakers whose work has quality, but who've never been able to attract a mass audience.

Back-End (noun/adj.): The amount of money left over from a movie's release after everyone has taken his/her cut, or a deal structured on such profits. Since profits tend to be highly elusive, even a small *front-end* deal is almost always better than a big *back-end* one.

Bean Counter (noun): A studio accountant.

Below the Line (adj.): Those elements of the film's budget that are principally technical in nature, such as crew (DP, grips, gaffers, etc.), the cost of sets, film stock, editing, sound mixing, special effects, etc. (*Ant.: Above-The-Line.*)

Boffo (adj.): Classic *Variety*ese for great or strong, usually used in reference to a film's performance at the box office. Used more frequently in print than in conversation.

Box-Office (noun): Literally, the place at which you buy tickets.

However, it's most often used to describe the amount of *money* a film makes over a particular period of time. Typical usage: The movie's weekend *box-office* was $15.3 million.

Buddy Movie (noun): A movie with two stars of the same sex; the characters often start out hating each other, but become friends in the end. *Lethal Weapon* is a classic buddy movie. *Thelma & Louise* is a female buddy movie.

Business, The (noun): The film and television industry. Anyone even remotely associated with mass-media entertainment, from the person who owns Sony Pictures to the girl who serves lunch on location, can claim to be in The Business. (*Syn.: The Industry.*)

Buzz (noun): A film's reputation *before* its actual release. From the time a screenplay hits the market through the finished film's final test screening, people will talk about it. Their reactions and prognostications, either good or bad, create the buzz.

C-List (noun): The theoretical list of actors and filmmakers who may be technically competent, but whose names carry little or no box-office weight. Ninety percent of the people in Hollywood are C-list. Thank God for good agents.

Castable (adj.): A movie with roles for A-list actors. "Buddy Movies" are usually very castable. A drama about 19th Century Australian aborigines would not be castable.

Character arc (noun): The change that a character experiences over the course of a story. Ebenezer Scrooge in Dickens' *A Christmas Carol* perhaps has modern literature's most famous character arc, from being a curmudgeonly miser to joyous philanthropist.

Chick Flick (noun): A film designed to attract a principally female audience. Chick Flicks tend to be about relationships and romance – as opposed to, say, blowing things up real good.

Coverage (noun): A report, usually two to four pages long, in which a screenplay's story is synopsized and an evaluation is made as to its commercial viability. Coverage usually stays on file forever, and bad coverage can haunt a script no matter how many rewrites it goes through. (Also, how a director chooses to shoot a scene, "Did you get the proper coverage?")

Crossover (noun): A film that allows a filmmaker known for attracting only a small, select audience to gain wider mainstream appeal.

D-Girl (noun): Short for Development Girl, this is Hollywood slang for anyone, male *or* female, who's on the lowest rungs of a studio or production company's development hierarchy. D-Girls – and they *are* principally female – are responsible for sifting through reader evaluations of new screenplays and determining whether or not to pass them along to their superiors.

Development (noun): The process of rewriting a screenplay, usually under a studio's guidance, and attaching those elements necessary to win a greenlight for production.

Development Hell (noun): The state of prolonged, seemingly endless rewriting. If your script has been in Development for more than six months, with no end in sight, you can comfortably claim to be in Development Hell.

Distributor (noun): The company responsible for making prints of a film, buying advertising, and physically getting the film into a movie theater. Most often, the major studios distribute the films they produce, as well as films produced by smaller, independent companies. In the case of a film co-produced by *two* studios – as was done with 1997's megahit *Titanic* – one company may be the *domestic* distributor, responsible for releasing the film in the United States and Canada, while the other studio handles distribution throughout the rest of the world.

Do Lunch (verb): The act of having lunch with a professional associate for the purpose of discussing business. Typical usage: "Let's *do lunch* Thursday."

E-Ticket (noun): During their first two decades, the Disney theme parks issued ticket booklets to its guests, allowing them to go on only a certain number of rides that were designated A through E. E-Ticket rides were the parks' best, like Space Mountain or Pirates of the Caribbean. Two decades later, movie folks still often refer to big, loud, expensive movies as E-Ticket movies, although many executives have no direct experience with this long-forgotten admissions practice.

Exhibitor (noun): A theater owner.

Element (noun): Any individual whose name and reputation add value to a project. An element is usually a big-name star, producer, director, or writer. Elements are what you attach to films in development.

Feel-Good (adj.): A movie with a happy ending; a film designed to be light, frothy, and not intellectually or emotionally challenging. Typical usage: "[This is] the *feel-good* movie of the year!"

Fish-Out-of-Water (adj.): A story about someone in an alien, unfamiliar environment.   Classic Fish-Out-Of-Water films include *Crocodile Dundee* and *Beverly Hills Cop*.

First-Look (noun/adj.): An arrangement by which a studio pays a production company X amount of dollars for the right to have first dibs on any project it creates. If the studio passes on the script, the producer is then free to shop it elsewhere.

Flavor-of-The-Month (noun): Usually a writer or director who's suddenly hot because of a recent hit movie or high-priced studio deal. Such heat can be very short-lived, so FOTMs are always advised to git while the gittin's good.

Franchise (noun): A series of popular films with continuing characters. The James Bond, *Star Wars*, *Star Trek*, *Batman* and *Lethal Weapon* movies are all examples of motion picture franchises.

Genre (noun): The type or category of story. For example, *Star Wars* is in the science fiction genre. *Big Daddy* is in the comedy genre. Often a film can represent a mix of genres. Examples: Action-comedy (*Beverly Hills Cop, Rush Hour*), romantic comedy (*While You Were Sleeping, My Best Friend's Wedding*) or science fiction-western (*Wild, Wild West*).

Greenlight (noun/verb): The order to actually produce a movie, or the act of doing so. Typical examples: "We finally got the *greenlight* for the movie;" "We could never get the studio honcho to *greenlight* the damn picture."

Gross (noun): The amount of money a film takes in at the box office. This is usually significantly higher than the amount of money a studio receives, since a film's gross must be shared with the exhibitor and/or the distributor.

Heat (noun): Excitement surrounding a motion picture project. Everyone wants to get involved with a movie that's got *heat*. (*Syn: Good Buzz.*)

High Concept (noun/adj.): A big commercial film whose story can be described in one or two simple sentences. *Jaws* was the first modern *high concept* film (man-eating shark terrorizes a tourist town), although the phrase itself wasn't coined until the 1980s, and was usually applied to Simpson/Bruckheimer productions (*Top Gun, Beverly Hills Cop, Flashdance*, etc.) and their ilk.

Hollywood (noun/adj.): Literally, a Los Angeles neighborhood northwest of downtown Los Angeles at the southern base of the Hollywood Hills. To most people, it means the entire motion picture and television industry. Hollywood is often used as an adjective, usually to describe a *type* of film (a feel-good movie aimed at the largest possible audience) or a lifestyle (expensive, flashy and hedonistic).

Honcho (noun): Slang for a studio chief. Different from the dated term "mogul," which usually referred not just to a studio chief, but also a studio *founder*.

Housekeeping Deal (noun): An arrangement by which a studio agrees to give a producer or production company office space on its lot, support services, and usually a modest operating budget in exchange for an exclusive or non-exclusive right to the projects he/they create.

Hyphenate (noun): Someone who performs multiple roles, such as a writer-producer-director.

Industry, The (noun): Another euphemism for the television and motion picture business. When you're in Southern California and you're talking about The Industry, you ain't talkin' about string beans or computer chips. (*Syn.: The Business*)

Legs (noun): A film's ability to earn money consistently. A film that grosses $15 million on its opening weekend, then only $7 million the next, does not have legs. A film that makes $10-$15 million week after week *does*.

Location (noun): Any place a film is shot that's not on a studio lot. If you shoot your film in China, you're on location. If you shoot a scene across the street from Paramount at the neighborhood deli, you're still on location. (*Ant.: "On the lot"* – *shooting on studio premises.*)

Log Line (noun): A one-or two-sentence description of a movie's plot. They're perfect for describing high concept plots (Example: *Air Force*

One – the President's plane gets hijacked by Russian terrorists.) But even more complex, character-driven stories must ultimately be reduced to this form. (Example: *Forrest Gump* – a simple but good-hearted Southerner pines for his childhood sweetheart while drifting through some of the most important historical events of the 1950s, '60s, and '70s. "It's *Rain Man* meets *Zelig!*")

Mogul (noun): Antiquated slang for studio chief, it's now the word most often used to describe the Founding Fathers of Hollywood. Largely second-generation European Jews, men like Louis B. Mayer, Sam Goldwyn, Harry Cohn, and Adolph Zuker were classic *moguls.*

Monkey Points (slang): The part of a studio contract that guarantees the participant a certain percentage of a film's revenues after a certain threshold, usually profitability, is reached. Since the studios' books are set up so that their films almost never show a profit, these points are offered just to stroke the filmmakers' ego.

Mouse, The (noun): Slang for the Walt Disney Co. Derived from its corporate symbol, Mickey Mouse.

Notes (noun): A memo from an authority figure listing criticisms and suggestions concerning a script in development. Notes generally come from producers, directors, or studio suits.

One-Sheet (noun): A movie poster. Often used to describe a single image that sells a movie. The *Jaws* poster, with its stark image of a shark zooming up on an unsuspecting swimmer, was a classic modern one-sheet.

On the Nose (adj.): Obvious or heavy-handed. Lacking subtlety or mystery, usually in conjunction with a movie's story development, character or dialogue.

Open (verb): To have a good box-office performance the first weekend in theatres. Typical usage: "The movie didn't even open." (Translation: The film did poorly on its first weekend.)

Package (noun/verb): A group of elements connected to a single project usually by a leading talent agency); the act of collecting elements for a film. An A-list star, an Oscar-winning director, and a famous screenwriter could constitute a movie's package.

Pass (verb): A polite euphemism for reject. No one in Hollywood has the balls to say, "Your script sucks." Instead they say, "I think were going to pass on this – but what else have you got?"

Post-Production (noun): The phase that follows *Production*, during which the film is assembled and made ready to show to the public. During Post-production, a film is edited, scored, sound effects are added, special effects are inserted, etc. A film's Post-production phase can often be significantly longer than its actual Production. (See *Pre-Production* and *Production*)

Pre-Production (noun): The phase of a movie's creation that occurs after Development, but before actual Production. For a movie to go into Pre-production, one first needs a greenlight from the studio. At that point, the key creative team is assembled, budgets are drawn up, the cast is chosen, and people plan just how and where they're going to shoot the movie. (See: *Production* and *Post-Production*)

Producer (noun): Can be anyone who has creative input on a movie, often without actually being involved in its physical production. Producers come in many forms and levels of clout:

Executive Producer – A high-profile filmmaker under whose auspices a movie is created. Executive Producers usually have little hands-on input, but attach their names in order to give a project credibility. (And take a nice fee for their efforts.) An Executive Producer can also be a financier (i.e., someone who raises the cash necessary to facilitate the budget).

Producer – Most often, the person responsible for initiating or finding a screenplay, getting a studio to finance it, hiring the director and key technical personnel, and overseeing every aspect of a film's development from rewriting to release. A Producer may work individually or in tandem with others of equal stature.

Co-Producer – Like a co-pilot, this person isn't quite on a par with the person he *co*'s with. Very often, a co-producer is the person who found or initiated a project, but who didn't have the personal clout to get a studio's backing. So he/she went to a Producer to get the project off the ground.

Associate Producer – Probably the most abused producer title around. An Associate Producer can be anyone who has had some degree of creative input on a project, but not very much actual responsibility. Writers who've had one or two successes often get an Associate Producer credit along with their proper screenplay title.

Line Producer – Of all the producer titles, this is probably the *most* specific. A Line Producer is the person responsible for overseeing the day-to-day running of a motion picture shoot. He/she tracks the budget, makes sure the sets are ready when they're needed, that crew and actors show up on time, etc.

Production (noun): The actual shooting phase of a movie, when actors speak their lines in front of a rolling camera. This is often the shortest part of a movie's creation. (See: *Pre-Production* and *Post-Production*.)

Property (noun): The basis of any motion picture project, usually a screenplay, a book, or even a licensed brand name.

Reader (noun): Someone paid a nominal sum to read and evaluate screenplays for an executive or studio. Readers have no power to say "Yes" to a purchase, but they can certainly say "No" and be listened to.

Rollercoaster (adj./noun): A phrase used to describe a fast-paced action/adventure film. *Star Wars* was the first modern roller-coaster movie, and has been followed over the past two decades by such roller-coaster blockbusters as *Raiders of the Lost Ark, Jurassic Park, Speed, Independence Day, Armageddon,* etc. (*Syn: E-Ticket*)

Schmooze (verb): Of Yiddish extraction, it means to engage in pleasant small talk with a business/creative associate. Typical usage: "We *schmoozed* for ten minutes, then started talking business."

Screening (noun): A private showing of a movie, usually for studio or industry insiders, or the press.

Shop (verb): No, not to buy things. It means to try to *sell* something, usually a screenplay or finished film. Typical usage: "We shopped the damn script all over town, but nobody bit."

Spec (noun): Short for speculative, usually refers to a screenplay written without any guarantee that it will ever be purchased. Can also refer to working in any capacity with only the *possibility* of pay down the line.

Suit (noun): A mid-level studio executive. Can refer to anyone from a creative director to a senior vice president. Usually noted for their conformist appearance, corporate demeanor, and endless profusion of notes.

Tank (verb): To do poorly at the box office. To bomb. Typical usage: "The film opened okay, but tanked in its second weekend."

Tentpole (noun): A big event movie around which a studio's seasonal release schedule is arranged. *Independence Day* was 20th Century Fox's tentpole movie for the summer of 1996. *Godzilla* served the same function for Sony in 1998.

Trades, The (noun): Literally trade or industry newspapers, usually used to refer to *Daily Variety* and *The Hollywood Reporter*.

Trailer (noun): In production, a vehicular dressing room, office space. Otherwise, a trailer is the coming attraction short that advertises a movie coming to a theater near you. Back in the Olden Days, these previews traditionally *followed* the main feature – hence the term trailer. Today, they always come *before* the main feature.

Turnaround (noun): A screen project that has been derailed by a studio during development and left to die; sometimes such projects may be offered for sale to competing studios. Typical usage: "After five rewrites, the studio gave up and put the picture in *turnaround*."

Web (noun): A major television network: CBS, ABC, NBC or Fox.

Weblet (noun): An upstart television network that may only provide programming for a handful of nights. UPN and the WB are currently *Weblets*. Fox grew from a *Weblet* in the 1980s into a full-fledged *Web* in the 1990s.

Wrap (noun/verb): Called after the last shot of a day's film production, or the act of finishing a shoot. Typical usage: "Cut! That's a wrap!"

Wrap Party (noun): A party held to celebrate the completion of a movie's shooting schedule.

Printed in the United States
70389LV00003B/1-111

9 780967 792606